PACK YOUR LUNCH

ALLAN DRAPER

PACK YOUR LUNCH

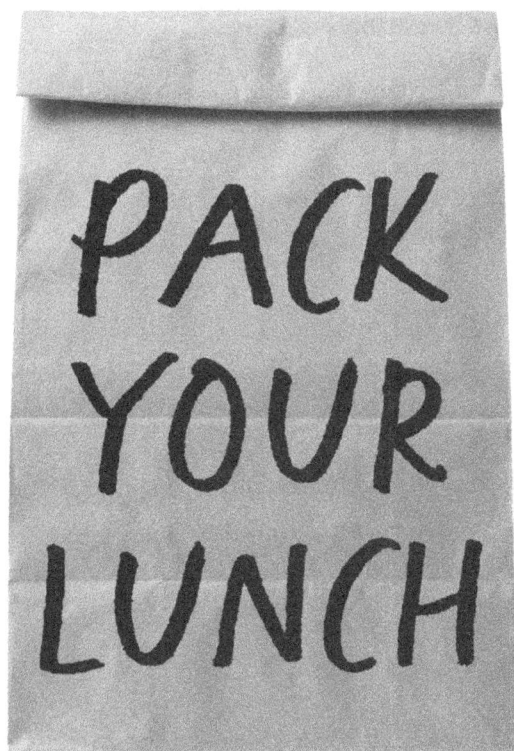

An Entrepreneur's Guide
to Mini Sacrifices That Lead
to Major Success

LIONCREST
PUBLISHING

PACK YOUR LUNCH
An Entrepreneur's Guide to Mini Sacrifices That Lead to Major Success

FIRST EDITION

ISBN   978-1-5445-4769-5   *Hardcover*
      978-1-5445-4768-8   *Paperback*
      978-1-5445-4770-1   *Ebook*

To Jules. You said "let's do it" when even I wasn't sure we should. That was the moment when everything changed.

CONTENTS

INTRODUCTION

"Great achievement is usually born of great sacrifice."

—NAPOLEON HILL

In 2014, I made a decision that changed my life forever. Driving home to Phoenix from a Valentine's Day weekend with my wife in Las Vegas, I got a call from my brother, Brent. He was leaving his partnership in the pest control business he had started. I didn't think much of it. After all, he and I had tried to start a similar business years earlier, but it hadn't worked out. We were young and immature, and the business was undercapitalized. Plus, we couldn't seem to get along. Since then, he had tried again and made it work, but now he and his partner had decided that it was better if they parted ways. I was sad to hear him say he was leaving the business behind.

In the meantime, I had gone back to school for a law degree and was building a new career as a practicing attorney. But my brother's phone call reignited something in me. Something that had existed before but had been tucked away. Maybe there's something similar inside of you.

Attempting to build that business together had been fun, even though it had failed. It was exciting. It was challenging. So I did something no one, including myself, expected: I tried to convince my brother to give it another go. Brent had the experience and knew what it would take. We were both more mature. And any personal issues that had sabotaged our earlier attempt could surely be put aside. My brother must have thought I was losing my marbles, because he did his best to talk me out of the idea. "Stick with the law," he said, "or you might regret it." To hear him talk, you'd think that starting and running a business was tougher than practicing law!

I kept after him, and by July, we were building a website and recruiting employees. Hiring our first door-to-door salesperson, Dion, was a sort of defining moment for me. "Wow," I thought, "We're really doing this—there's no backing out, no quitting now!" I was filled with nervousness and excitement. My family's livelihood would depend on my success, but by hiring an employee, I was responsible for someone else's livelihood too. That responsibility was the first point of no return. I had to move forward, and the business had to succeed.

Little did I know that I'd have many more moments like that in the weeks, months, and years to come. I had no idea that what started out as one hire and one company would become, over the years, hundreds of employees and dozens of companies. I also hadn't considered the risks I would have to take and sacrifices I'd have to make on my way to becoming a serial entrepreneur. Or that with each decision, risk, and sacrifice, I would become more committed to the business. In some ways, I'm glad I didn't know what it would be like because if I had, it's possible I never would have started. But deep down, I knew I was going to build something, and nothing was going to stop me.

There was the moment I quit my job as a lawyer. And when I packed up my house and all my family's belongings and moved my wife and kids across the country from Phoenix to Detroit. Each step in the progression felt like burning a boat, and so no matter what happened, I couldn't go back. It was sink or swim time, and it was terrifying.

I could have been overwhelmed with fear. *Fears.* What if I couldn't provide for my family? That was the big one. But there were a lot more. If I failed and had to go back to the law, how would I explain the gap in my résumé? And what would I tell people—my friends, relatives, and former colleagues? Earlier, when our business hadn't succeeded, I could blame a lot of things. I was young and inexperienced back then, too immature to start a company. But now I was all grown up. I was a *lawyer*. Failure wasn't acceptable.

Getting deeper into the startup, part of me wanted to retreat to the safety of the law practice. That part was saying, "What are you thinking? You have an education, a good job, and a great life. Do you really want to risk it all for a bug company?" But another part of me wanted to build something—to control my own destiny. The trailblazer within me knew that if I didn't at least give this business thing a try, I would regret it for the rest of my life—and that even if it didn't work out, the sting of failure wouldn't come close to the pain and disappointment of not trying.

Burning the boats—making and taking those irreversible decisions and actions—was painful but necessary. Without doing that, at the first sign of trouble, it would have been too easy to return to my old job. But it was also liberating. With every boat burned and every lifesaver cast aside, I was also letting go of responsibilities that had been holding me back from becoming the person I wanted to be. These were just a few of the sacrifices I would have to make—the mini sacrifices every entrepreneur who's serious about starting a business *must* make.

Every entrepreneur gets to a point where they ask themselves, "Hey, is this going to be worth it to me or not?" I struggled with that question and an even bigger one: "Am I even capable of doing this?" That question would come up again and again. Whatever business you're starting, or thinking about starting, you probably have the same questions and concerns. Like me, you're afraid of what it will take and whether you're up to it. You don't want to let yourself down, especially if other people are counting on you. I see you. I *was* you.

I was mostly worried about how my decision would affect my family. But even if you're single and no one depends on you financially or in other ways, starting a new venture still comes with risks. Unless you're independently wealthy or living in your mom's basement, you still have to support yourself. And you have relationships with other people who count on your time and friendship.

You're worried about what will happen if you fail too. How will you start over? What will people say about you? And how will it affect the people you care about? And if you succeed, how will that affect you and everyone else? Either way, you're going to have to make sacrifices.

MINI SACRIFICES FOR MAJOR SUCCESS

Sacrifices are absolutely necessary. You're going to have to make a lot of them, and I will explain each sacrifice, chapter by chapter, in this book. These mini sacrifices are essential to major business success. They're also essential for supporting a healthier, happier, more purpose-driven life as you launch, scale, and operate your business today and for as long as you are a business owner.

You will have to sacrifice financial stability—at least for a while.

You'll have to get comfortable with risk, conflict, and stress.

You'll have less time for hobbies, sports, and other people, including family and friends.

You'll have to get used to feeling alone, vulnerable, and occasionally out of control.

You will have to become more flexible with your identity.

You'll have to face your worst fears.

You will fail. Yes, you'll fail, probably many times, but it won't be as bad as you think.

These mini sacrifices will make you a better, stronger, more resilient entrepreneur, but only *if* you know how to manage them. Because sacrificing the wrong things can destroy you. You could damage or even lose what matters most—parts of your life that are more important than your business.

Making the right sacrifices, on the other hand, empowers you by liberating you from activities, weaknesses, and distractions that can prevent you from being the successful entrepreneur you want to be. The right sacrifices put you in control of your destiny. And for every sacrifice that you make, there is an enormous reward just around the corner—a major reward that is impossible to achieve without the corresponding sacrifice.

―――

For every sacrifice that you make, there is an enormous reward just around the corner—a major reward that is impossible to achieve without the corresponding sacrifice.

―――

New business owners are afraid of what they don't know—what it will be like if and when they ever get this business ownership thing figured out. They don't know what they don't know, and that's scary. Sound familiar? Join the club. When you're starting a business, all the unexpected sacrifices you have to make—not to mention the ones looming ahead—sort of hit you all at once. They can paralyze you if you let them. Since starting dozens of businesses, I've learned a thing or two about sacrifices.

First, sacrifices are unavoidable. You have to make them.

Second, most sacrifices aren't as painful as you think. But you must understand what you're giving up and be intentional about the ones you make. This means identifying the nonnegotiables, building a wall around them, and protecting them. Some sacrifices should never be made, especially those that cannot be repaired or replaced.

Third, some of the sacrifices you make are going to hurt, at least at first. But in the end, they'll make you a stronger, wiser, and happier business owner. They will give you more control over your business and your life. Making sacrifices will lead you to achieve things when avoiding them never could.

Whether you're getting ready to start a business, months into your first business, or juggling several of them, unless you understand and manage the mini sacrifices necessary to succeed, you'll struggle to get any traction or scale. This will affect your business, your relationships—even your health.

Business owners who fail to make these sacrifices struggle at every stage. They might be new to business ownership, or they've started a business (or two, or three) but can't seem to get any traction. They're feeling overwhelmed and wondering what they're doing wrong. The competition makes it look so easy. It's enough to make a struggling business owner ask, "What do they know that I don't?"

Most new business owners have no idea what they're getting into. Nobody told them that mini sacrifices are necessary for major success. Often, when they realize what's required, they don't want to do the work. Specifically, they don't want to make the sacrifices. It's no wonder that, according to 2024 data from the US Bureau of Labor Statistics, 20.4 percent of businesses fail in their first year after opening, 49.4 percent fail in their first five years, and a whopping 65.3 percent fail in their first ten years.[1]

But those aren't the businesses you hear about. You only hear about the successes, or those that *appear* to be successes. It's easy to convince yourself that everyone but you has it all figured out, when nothing could be further from the truth. In reality, most people, including me, walk with faith from struggle to struggle. We look like we have all the answers, but in reality, we just have what it takes to keep searching for them. And a big part of those answers is making the right sacrifices.

> Most people, including me, walk with faith from struggle to struggle. We look like we have all the answers, but in reality, we just have what it takes to keep searching for them.

1   "What Percentage of Small Businesses Fail? 2024 Data Reveals the Answer," Commerce Institute, accessed November 14, 2024, https://www.commerceinstitute.com/business-failure-rate/.

I had to make many sacrifices, but the decisions I made helped my business succeed. More importantly, they helped me grow as an entrepreneur, a partner, a husband, a father, and a man. That's what I hope for you too, and what I believe is possible.

You might not be ready for my advice. We entrepreneurs aren't always good at listening to other people. We don't color inside the lines and follow all the rules. We like doing things our own way. So you're coming into this book thinking, "What the heck does this guy know that I don't?"

I'm going to ask you to think differently. Don't accept my advice blindly (as if you would) and follow it in lockstep. Think of me as a serial entrepreneur who's come to terms with the sacrifices I had to make for success. If you're open to hearing me out, you might just learn something that you can apply to your own situation.

That way, you can make your own decisions. You don't have to go into this whole business thing kicking and screaming and feeling like you're being forced to conform. You can do things your way, with more insight into what to expect so you won't be blindsided and can make decisions that are right for your business but also won't ruin your life. Among all the fear and anxiety, there's plenty of room for optimism and hope. I believe in you, and I want you to believe in yourself too.

PACK YOUR LUNCH

Think of these sacrifices as packing your lunch versus grabbing fast food. Packing your lunch takes time, planning, and patience. You have to buy the bread and the sandwich fixings, or whatever you choose to eat, ahead of time. You have to spend a few minutes in the morning—between getting dressed, eating breakfast, and rushing out the door—putting it all together. How much easier it is to simply wait until lunchtime and then grab a quick burger and fries. In the short term, packing your lunch is a small sacrifice of time and money. But in the long run, it will cost less and take less time. You'll end up with a healthier, more affordable, and better-tasting meal that won't give you heartburn, drain your wallet, or have you loosening your belt (or worse, taking a nap) by three o'clock. This is why packing your lunch—making mini sacrifices, especially for new entrepreneurs—is essential for long-term business growth and success.

Like packing your lunch, building a business also takes time, planning, and patience. Think of it like the meme of the guy digging for diamonds, wondering how long he'll have to dig to hit the jewels. A business owner could be inches from the diamonds when, suddenly, they give up. If only they had kept digging just a little longer! When you start a business, you have to do a lot of digging to get to the gems. And even when you reach the diamonds, you still have to keep digging because owning a business isn't the prize at the end. It's a continuous journey that never ends until you sell the business or shut it down. But being the business owner—that's the payoff. Building it, scaling it, dealing with the issues, and making it a success is worth more than all the diamonds in the world.

If you're like me, you'll realize that starting a business really *is* harder than practicing law or whatever job you gave up to be an entrepreneur. But you will also learn that the rewards of doing so will be more numerous than you can now imagine.

If you read this book and follow my advice, you will have a better idea of what's required to be successful. You'll realize that a lot of things you're dreading will actually make your life better. You'll look forward to packing your lunch and enjoying the rewards. Then you can face your sacrifices head-on and make them intentionally, giving yourself the time, money, and energy you need to focus on those things that matter most, including your business.

Let's talk about those sacrifices again:

You will have to sacrifice financial stability—at least for a while.

This is true, especially at first, and maybe for years. When I started my business, I thought I'd have more time, money, and freedom right away. It doesn't work that way. In fact, I had to give up time, money, and freedom in the short term in order to achieve those long-term benefits I was seeking.

You'll have to get comfortable with risk, conflict, and stress.

Risk, conflict, and stress are synonymous with entrepreneurism. But you don't have to let them take you down.

You'll have less time for hobbies, sports, and other people, including family and friends.

By prioritizing your life's categories, you'll protect what matters most and discover you've been wasting precious time, money, and energy on people and things that were never really important to you in the first place.

You'll have to get used to feeling alone, vulnerable, and occasionally out of control.

New entrepreneurs expect to feel confident, powerful, popular, and in control. Actually, the opposite is true, especially early on. It's all part of the job, my friend.

You will have to become more flexible with your identity.

This isn't as weird as it sounds. I'm not going to ask you to change your name or the color of your hair. I am going to ask you to get out of your own head and learn to see yourself from others' perspectives— and maybe make some changes that help you, your business, and the people around you.

You'll have to face some of your worst fears.

Spoiler alert: they're not as bad as you think, not even the worst ones.

You will fail.

Yes, you'll fail, probably many times. In order to eventually succeed, failures are inevitable. But just like your fears, they will be less painful than you imagine. It won't feel that way when you're in the middle of one, but your failures are your best opportunities for growth.

The funny thing (okay, maybe it's not so funny) is that while you're conquering all these demons and making strides in your business, everyone around you will see the successes. Meanwhile, all you'll see is what's left to do. That's natural—it's how we entrepreneurs are made. We're always looking ahead, so much so that we forget to celebrate our accomplishments. So while everyone else sees us as wildly successful business owners, we're stressed out, anxious, and some days, a little angry. No matter how well we're doing, we always feel as if we should be doing better.

WE ARE ALL WORKS IN PROGRESS

When I started my first business, I didn't understand any of this. Straight out of BYU, I thought it would be easy. But like I said, I was young, immature, and undercapitalized, and my business partner, my brother, Brent, and I didn't get along. Looking back, that's really no surprise. The pressures we put on ourselves were enough to upset any relationship. For a while, I gave up on my vision of being an entrepreneur. I went to law school, graduated, and got a job. The phone call from my brother on that fateful Valentine's Day weekend revived something in me. Suddenly, all those old feelings rose to the surface, and I couldn't get the idea out of my head: I knew that, in my heart, I was an entrepreneur, and I had to try again. This time around—older, wiser, and with some money in the bank—I wasn't just going to wing it and hope for the best. I was committed to making the business a success.

That company took off, and so I started another one, and another, and eventually a law practice. As I write this book, I've founded over twenty businesses, I've hired over a thousand people, and I have hundreds of employees on the payroll. My companies run the gamut in industries from home services, financial lending, angel and real estate investing, software, and product and brand development to digital marketing, coaching, and podcasting.

None of this happened overnight. At times, I suffered from a lack of confidence, even imposter syndrome. It seemed like everyone thought I knew what I was doing, and I was tasked with meeting their expectations. If you've had an accountability partner, you know how that feels. Imagine having a hundred accountability partners. That's what it felt like. If only those people had known what was going on inside my head and my heart.

I became an expert in a few industries, but my real superpower was starting businesses. Like many entrepreneurs, I'm a big idea person—a visionary. I can put the right people, money, ideas, and other resources together to create a business. From there, I can hand it to someone else to run at the operational level.

Don't get me wrong—I'm not a know-it-all. I may sound full of confidence, but it comes in waves. I still consider myself a work in progress. I still suffer from severe imposter syndrome. Part of me feels as if I just got lucky and don't really belong in this position. Yet here I am. Another part of me looks back at what it took to get here and knows I absolutely belong.

I belong here, and you belong here too.

This book started as a way to label my fears and emotions. I wanted to understand everything I had gone through to get here. Not the strategic, operational, or tactical work of being a business owner, but the stuff no one talks about. The really hard decisions I had to make about what to protect and what to sacrifice on my way to becoming a business owner. I realized that the feelings I experienced with each new business repeated themselves over and over. There was a pattern that told me my emotions weren't a one-off experience. After speaking with many other business owners, I realized they weren't unique to me either. Everyone went through the same thing.

This is where my law training actually paid off. As a society, we try to create laws that apply to every scenario, but that's not possible. So we have to look for commonalities. Eventually, we see patterns. As a lawyer, you don't just learn "the law"; you study cases from all over the US and look for patterns. Among the different fact sets, you identify the commonalities. You see if the fact set for your case shares those commonalities and decide whether the same laws apply. I apply the same technique to starting businesses—look for the commonalities, see the patterns, apply the lessons. This gives me a unique perspective among entrepreneurs, but it's something I believe I can share to help them overcome their own struggles, which are a lot like mine.

THE CHOICE IS YOURS

Whether you decide to make these sacrifices is up to you. I've worked with a lot of new business owners who failed to do what was necessary. The outcomes usually went one of three ways:

1. They didn't understand what they would have to give up, and when they felt as if they were giving up too much, they gave up on their business and went back to their old career. (This is the most common.)
2. They resented the sacrifices they would have to make, so they went in the opposite direction and sacrificed nothing. That wasn't sustainable, and their business failed or at least failed to grow.
3. They became so focused on their business, sacrificed the wrong things, and didn't allow time, money, or energy for anything else. They succeeded at being business owners but failed at everything else—including their health, happiness, and relationships.

I've helped entrepreneurs turn their businesses around and coached business owners to succeed. In every case, they had to adopt a different perspective on sacrifices and be willing to make them. Being a business owner requires abandoning the "today or next day at the latest" attitude and adopting a long-term view and the patience, stamina, and diligence to get there. It means packing your lunch instead of pulling into the drive-up at the local fast-food joint. It's for people who are in it for the long run.

In that respect, this book is not for people who want to start a business and then close it or sell it next year. It's not for people who want to start a business and never scale. It's not necessarily for solopreneurs, either, though many of the lessons apply to solopreneurs and people who might want to sell their business several years down the road. But if that's your *main* focus, this book is not for you.

This book is not an operations manual for starting or running a business. I won't tell you how to register your LLC with the state, set up a website, or create a profit and loss statement. We're not going over the stuff you learn in business school. What I have to tell you isn't taught in classrooms or the topic of conversation in masterminds and retreats. It's the ugly, scary, weird stuff no one wants to talk about because they think they're the only one going through it, and, oh no, what if everyone else found out? Face it: everyone goes through this stuff. I do, and every business owner who's been honest enough to open up will tell you they have too. You might think you're immune, but it doesn't work that way. Until you're in the middle of starting and running a business, you won't see a lot of this stuff coming.

This book is not a checklist either. It's a guide, and you're going to want to color outside the lines. You'll want to make your own rules, and I hope you do. No one can tell you what matters to you, and no one can tell you how to start and run a business. It's different for everyone, including you.

If you want to start a business, this book is about what's holding you back. It fills in the gap between where you are now and where you want to be.

If you have a business and are ready to give up, it's about all those things you didn't see coming that are hitting you squarely in the face and what you can do about them.

If you have several businesses, are overwhelmed, and feel like you're sacrificing too much and are struggling to grow, it's about what's taking too much of your time, money, and energy and preventing you from taking that next big step.

And if you are any of these people, it's a book that will help you understand the sacrifices necessary to being a business owner so you can be judicious about each one and take control of your critical limited resources: time, money, and energy.

This book is about how sacrifices are not the big, scary things that will take you and your business down. Viewed from a different lens, these mini sacrifices are massive opportunities to gain more than you ever thought was possible. Think of them as hacks to shortcut your success.

Have you heard of the Stanford marshmallow experiment? Children were offered one marshmallow and were told that if they waited to eat it, they would be given another. The researcher then left each child in the room alone with the marshmallow for about fifteen minutes. Later studies showed that the children who waited for the second marshmallow had "better life outcomes." These results were determined by SAT scores, educational attainment, body mass index (BMI), and other life measures.[2]

This book is for people willing to make mini sacrifices and put off immediate gratification for something greater in the future. It's for people willing to not immediately eat that first marshmallow—people willing to take a few minutes to pack their lunch in the morning.

This is a personal journey—my journey and yours. Every entrepreneur's journey is unique, following whatever path it needs to take to fulfill the individual's goals. Likewise, my solution isn't tidy and streamlined, but it's flexible. It's what must be faced head-on, regardless of the business.

You know that one guy in class who always raises his hand and asks the stupid question? Everyone else just sort of rolls their eyes as if they can't believe he doesn't know the answer. But secretly, none of them knows the answer, and they're really glad he asked it, because they never would. Well, I'm going to be that guy. We're going to talk about all that stuff everyone pretends isn't a problem, even though every single entrepreneur is dealing with it.

Are you ready?

Of course you are.

---

2   Angel E. Navidad, "Stanford Marshmallow Test Experiment," Simply Psychology, last updated September 7, 2023, https://www.simplypsychology.org/marshmallow-test.html.

1

THERE WILL BE SACRIFICES

"The things that seem difficult, that seem like sacrifices, are the vehicles to an easier life. The paradox is there is no such thing as a sacrifice. There are only short-term down payments on rich future blessings."

—RORY VADEN

I graduated from high school in 1998. After two years of college, I considered doing a two-year mission for my church. Naturally, I worried about what I would be giving up: essentially delaying everything typical nineteen-year-olds do, like working to earn money, continuing my college studies, dating girls, attending concerts and sporting events, and enjoying time with my family and friends.

My high school seminary teacher told me, "The mission is not actually a sacrifice because you get more out of it than you give up." I remembered those wise words as I was making the decision about whether I should go. Still, I wasn't convinced. The more I thought about what my friends would be doing, the more I struggled with my decision. No girls. No movies. No TV or music. But again, I would be doing it for the Church. Also, I'd be helping people who didn't have the luxury of a typical American lifestyle.

The mission wouldn't only prevent me from making money, but it would actually cost money. I would have to pay for the whole trip, and I couldn't choose the location where I would serve or even know where I was going until after the paperwork was complete. I saw the mission as a major sacrifice. But I believed that teaching about Jesus was a worthwhile venture, despite what I was giving up.

Ultimately, I chose to go, and after a very long application process, I was on my way to Utah for a ten-week crash course in Spanish and being a missionary. My ultimate destination would be South America—Viña del Mar, Chile, to be exact.

Back then, missions were more rigid than they are today. Missionaries could not use cell phones or the internet. They spoke to their families only twice a year, on Mother's Day and Christmas. During my first year, I had just one call because I was in the missionary training center, with no telephone, on the first Mother's Day.

I didn't know anyone at the training center or in Chile. That's how it worked. They didn't send friends together. On that first bus ride in Chile, I listened closely to the locals and thought, "Did I learn the wrong language?" The dialect sounded nothing like the textbook Spanish taught at the training center.

Though none of my church friends were there, I recognized a few people from the training center. I was assigned a companion—someone who stuck by my side at all times, except when I went to the bathroom. So there was no privacy. That took some getting used to.

But I got used to it. They kept me busy working for the Church six days a week, proselytizing in the local community, and helping members of the Church. The locals didn't have much. Some homes were no more than a collection of sticks with a dirt floor. One day a week was a service day, where I'd help out in the community by doing physical labor such as yard work and cleaning up after floods. Repairing a roof, I fell through the roof up to my thighs. More than once, I thought about what the seminary teacher had said, that I would get more than I gave. How, exactly, was falling through a thatched roof and shoveling mud helping me? Other than sore arms, scraped up legs, and a backache, I couldn't see the benefit.

Something happened over those two years, though. My perspective changed. I changed. I expected these poor people to be miserable. They weren't. They were happy, and they appreciated everything we did for them. They saw the world in a different way, and I began to see it that way too.

I realized that twenty-year-old me had been focused on myself. I did things that benefited me directly, thinking that would make me happy, would make me better, would make me a man. But just this brief period of my life, this small sacrifice, was doing much more. I felt differently about other people. More connected. More responsible for their outcomes. My mission in Chile made me a better person. Later, it made me a better husband and father. I have friendships from those years that will last a lifetime. Looking back, I know that teacher was right: I got much more than I gave. My mission was indeed a blessing disguised as a sacrifice.

That lesson stuck with me. It's seen me through a lot of tough times, like when I began to resent the sacrifices I was making for my businesses. I had to remind myself to consider what I was giving up and what I would get in return.

Starting a business comes with sacrifices. That sounds scary. You're giving something up—changing your current way of life and moving away from the status quo. It took a long time to get where you are; why would you want any of it to change?

Think about sacrifices like this: they are true sacrifices only if what you give up matters more than what you receive in return. By that definition, the sacrifices I'm asking you to make in this book aren't true sacrifices. They're investments in yourself, your business, and your future.

> Think about sacrifices like this: they are true sacrifices only if what you give up matters more than what you receive in return.

I'm going to ask you to make difficult decisions and take actions that are different from what you're doing today. I'm going to call them sacrifices because that's what they'll feel like in the moment. Over time, as they pay off, you'll see them for what they are: the only way to survive and succeed as an entrepreneur.

START WITH THE NONNEGOTIABLES

To help you figure out whether the sacrifice is worth it, you will have to consider your nonnegotiables. These are those things in life that matter most. Your health, your friends, and your family, for example. Maybe your dog. Your nonnegotiables are untouchable. As a business owner, you have to identify them early on so you never, ever sacrifice them.

Say your nightly routine is eating ten Oreos before bed. If I asked you to quit doing that, it would feel like a sacrifice. You're giving up something that makes you feel good at the moment. But you'd probably lose some weight (mostly fat), and your dentist would thank you. So you're not really making a sacrifice. You're changing your behavior—even though not having those cookies is painful at first—for the long-term benefits.

Clearly, Oreos are not nonnegotiables. Other parts of your life are. You have to identify and prioritize them, then commit to not sacrificing them, no matter what. This might seem odd—why would anyone do something that impacts their family in a negative way? Until you're running a business, you don't know how far you'll be stretched and how easy it will be to overstep those boundaries. That's why it's so important to consider them now, while you're thinking clearly and not in the middle of dealing with employees, customers, and the bank.

THE NONNEGOTIABLES WITHIN MY LIFE'S SEVEN CATEGORIES

Your nonnegotiables are different from mine and everyone else's. They are what matter most to you. However, you'll probably find commonalities between yours and mine. I identify my nonnegotiables by first categorizing the seven main areas of my life in order of priority.

1. **God/Spiritual.** Your number 1 might be a different religion, the Universe, a Higher Power, or whatever you believe spiritually. Or it could be something completely different. For all I know, your number 1 could be pickleball. I don't judge. The important thing here is to really think about what matters most to you.
2. **Family.** For me, this is my immediate family—my wife and kids. Your family might comprise other members of your family, your closest friends, and your pets. Categories are personal and unique, so you and no one else get to decide what they are.
3. **Mental and emotional health.** I define this as how I feel about myself and my mental fortitude. Am I generally happy? Am I in a good place with how I feel about myself? Am I continuing to grow? Can I do hard things?
4. **Physical health.** We business owners are prone to overwork, which can devastate our bodies. I'm proactive about keeping myself from being sick, tired, or in pain.
5. **Profession.** This category encompasses my businesses and me as a business owner. Are my businesses growing? Am I improving as a businessperson? This category—essentially, *work*—can become an addiction. It can consume you, affecting your other life categories. Therefore, get your categories sorted out and prioritized now, before you're so busy you don't realize how your life is changing, and not necessarily for the better. If you have to sacrifice some-

thing to put in those long hours, make sure it's in a category that's lower on the list.

6. **Finances.** I can do well within my profession and still not reach my financial goals, so I separate number 5 and number 6. I want to earn enough to grow my businesses while having enough left over for other parts of my life, such as family vacations and financial investments. Notice that I prioritize "profession" above "finances." I'll explain why in a minute.

7. **Social life.** This includes my friends and my community.

The first four categories—God, family, and mental and emotional health, and physical health—are my nonnegotiables. Categories 5 and 6, "profession" and "finances," are particularly relevant to the main topic of this book—making short-term sacrifices to start, run, and build a profitable business. The key is to let nothing lower on the list disrupt the higher categories. If you think it might, weigh your choices. A decision that furthers your professional career (number 5) or finances (number 6) may impact your soul (number 1), family (number 2), or health (number 3 and number 4) from which you can't recover.

To help you prioritize, think about where you want to be in five, ten, even twenty years. Create a vision board representing these future stages of your business and life. A lot of times, it's the shortsightedness or the "need it now" mentality that creates a gray area for our priorities. So you have to identify your priorities and "pack your lunch." Otherwise, you'll be tempted to give in to burgers and fries later.

Prioritization matters not only with regard to the nonnegotiables, but throughout the categories. For example, staying in a dead-end job that pays well may advance your financial situation (number 6), but what is it doing to your professional self (number 5)? This is why I prioritize profession over finances. Not to mention how staying in a career with no future affects numbers 1 through 4.

Rarely will a decision or action in a category impact only that category. So you have to consider how it affects the others, especially the ones that matter the most. If your decisions within the less important categories have a negative impact on those of higher importance, especially the nonnegotiables, then you are making a real sacrifice. Real sacrifices deliver less than you give up, and they lead to a negative outcome.

This might sound a little too analytical, but if you come up with your own categories and prioritize them, then consider examples of each one, you'll see how easy it can be to keep your priorities in check and ensure you're not making bad decisions. However, being a business owner comes with a truckload of new responsibilities. You're going to be so busy that you'll forget about those priorities. They may be nagging at you in the back of your mind, but when you're really busy, you'll be tempted to push them aside. That's why you need to keep them front and center. Write them down. Put them on a whiteboard. Hang them in your office. Frame them and put them on your desk. Don't lose sight of them. My vision board includes all my categories, and every morning I revisit it, imaging myself and my business five or ten years down the road. I ask myself how I'll feel then about the choices I'm making today. Specifically, how will today's actions impact my nonnegotiables in the future?

I'm telling you this now because losing sight of those nonnegotiables will happen. It happened to me. It's happened to every business owner I know. Being aware of what matters most in your life and knowing your time, resources, and attention will be spread thin empowers you to get ahead of the challenges now and can help you avoid making real sacrifices.

REAL-LIFE NONNEGOTIABLE DECISIONS

I'll give you some examples of decisions I've made within my life's categories. At the end of this chapter, I'll ask you to make your own list of categories, prioritize them, identify your nonnegotiables, and come up with your own examples.

1. **God/Spiritual.** We all have a moral code, whether it's established by our upbringing, religion, education, experiences, or a combination of these factors. Doing something unethical, immoral, or dishonest—anything that goes against those deep beliefs that make me the person I am—violates my number 1 category. I might be tempted to cut corners with one of my businesses to make more money. But since cutting corners shortchanges my customers, which is unethical, and since "finances" is down there at number 6, that's a no-go. See how easy this is? You might think, "Hey, Allan, I would never shortchange my customers. That's just common sense!" But common sense becomes less common when you're starting a business and juggling a million things and under a lot of pressure. That's why you have to figure this stuff out, write it down, and never forget it.

2. **Family.** It's five o'clock on Friday, and there's so much more work to do. Should I stay until eight and miss dinner with the kids? Skip out on date night with my wife? What would you do? Again, a lot of this is common sense. It's just not so common at the end of a busy day. I'll have more to say about this in Chapter 5, "Your Relationships Will Change."

3. **Mental and emotional health.** Some days, being a business owner tries my last nerve. It's difficult, complicated, and stressful. My bank doesn't always follow my instructions. My people don't always do their jobs. My customers don't all give me five-star reviews. I can allow myself to be frustrated, angry, and upset, but I can't allow those feelings to linger and affect my mental and emotional health. I'll have more on the subject in Chapter 7, "Your Life Will Have Conflict," and Chapter 8, "Your Stress Will Increase."

4. **Physical health.** Physical exercise and a sensible diet are often the first sacrifices a new business owner makes. When I skip a workout or eat something I shouldn't, the short-term effects are obvious. I feel lousy. But the hidden long-term effects of not exercising and eating a poor diet, day after day, are much worse. That lifestyle could take years off my life. Allowing my health to decline also

impacts all my other life categories. In fact, how well I manage each of the seven categories impacts all the others to a degree.

5. **Profession.** The professional category includes everything to do with my businesses and my career as a business owner. An example of a good long-term sacrifice here is making a decision that will be a sacrifice financially in the short term but helps me further my professional goals, such as paying $13,000 to a brand builder that pays off with a more recognizable brand and increased revenue. On the other hand, taking on too many businesses, which affects my stress level, may not be a good choice.

6. **Finances.** Excessive spending, especially to impress other people, is a common problem among new business owners. It's a trap I've been able to avoid. I like to buy nice things (I have a penchant for cars) but not if those purchases affect the five previous categories.

7. **Social life.** I tend to neglect this category, which is a shame, because I have some fantastic friends. Fortunately, my wife is in tune with my moods, and when I'm feeling stressed out, she'll say, "Why don't you go out and do something with your buddies?" This is the kind of advice I need to hear when I need to hear it. Business owners can spend a lot of time alone, which we'll get into in Chapter 10, "You Will Have to Become Okay with Feeling Alone," and we have to be intentional about spending time with other people.

How you define and prioritize your categories is a guide—it's not a hard-and-fast rule. If my office is on fire and putting it out means missing my kid's baseball practice, I'm going to put out the fire. The seven categories have to work in harmony so I can be the person I want to be for myself and the people who matter the most while also running a successful business.

Occasionally, you might make a decision that prioritizes a category that's less important. When this happens, remember to be kind to yourself. Acknowledge it, reassess your commitment to your true priorities, and show yourself some mercy. This can be an art more than a science.

IDENTIFYING YOUR CATEGORIES

Think about the different categories in your life. Are the most import-ant ones getting the attention they deserve? Are you spending too much time on the ones that don't matter as much? Most people know the answers to these questions intuitively, but if you need help, look at where you're spending your resources—your time and money. If you keep a calendar, where are you spending most of your time? You have to spend a lot of time working, but what about the rest of the day? Is it going toward your higher priorities or something else? Now check out your bank statement. Where is your money going?

To be clear, mortgage payments put a roof over your family's head. Groceries keep them alive. Even if you're single, paying for a home and food keeps you safe and alive. Likewise, sports equipment, swimming lessons, and recreational fees are probably dollars well spent and might count toward the family, physical health, and mental health categories. A weekly golf game with your friends counts toward the social category, but if you don't also have a weekly date with your significant other, is it worth it? Think about the categories that benefit the most from your resources and where they sit on your list.

Are you happy with what you see? Or was this exercise a wake-up call?

PRIORITIZE YOUR LIFE FOR PERSONAL ALIGNMENT AND PROFESSIONAL SUCCESS

Entrepreneurs who skip identifying what matters, especially the non-negotiables, and prioritizing each category can get into trouble in a lot of ways. They see their business and relationships suffering and cheat or take shortcuts to adjust. I've seen business owners commit fraud, turn to addiction, and have extramarital affairs due to a mis-alignment between their resources and their priorities. They justify their behavior with excuses like "I work so hard; I deserve a break," or "Look at what I've accomplished. I deserve a little leeway." We've seen business owners like this—visionaries we looked up to who suddenly lost their way. They sacrificed the wrong things and feel out of alignment.

Sacrifices are a required part of the business ownership journey, but when you sacrifice what matters less for what matters more, the outcome outweighs what you give up. Choosing which sacrifices to make is critically important now because when you go from being an employee to owning the company, the demands on your resources explode. It's easy to lose sight of what's important, and so you have to identify and protect those things while sacrificing those things in your life that you are willing to let go.

Entrepreneurs often justify poor sacrifices. We buy into the notion that our worth is defined by our work and productivity. We put in long hours and tell ourselves we're doing it to make ourselves more valuable. We convince ourselves that we're working to ensure our family's financial stability, when in truth, we're doing it for ourselves. There's nothing wrong with working hard for yourself, but be honest about your motivations. Given the choice, your family would probably have more of your time. That's not to say you won't have to work a lot, because you will. But you have to be aware of how it affects your nonnegotiables.

Look for opportunities to combine activities in your life's categories. I'm not talking about multitasking, but doing things that satisfy objectives in more than one of your life's areas. For example, when my son became interested in golf, I was thrilled. Golf is an activity that's good for my physical and mental health; playing it while spending time with one of my favorite people satisfies three of my nonnegotiables. I don't track this stuff in a spreadsheet, but I am aware of it, and whenever I can do something that ticks off more than one category, I'm all in.

When we reframe what we see as sacrifices, we see the benefit of making small sacrifices for something greater. Recognizing what's most important in our lives requires introspection. Our nonnegotiables are unique to us. Your categories and how you prioritize them may be different from mine. There is no guidebook for how many hours we should spend at work, at home, or going to the gym. We have to conduct a sort of self-analysis and think deeply to determine what really counts. How we spend our time varies from person to person and even from week to week. We have to look at our bank statements and calendars to see whether our assets are being allocated in accordance with our priorities. Aligning our resources and priorities is the sacrifice we must make, as people, and especially as business owners whose responsibilities grow as our resources are stretched thin, at least at first. This will change as we scale our businesses, make more money, have more time, and delegate work to employees.

Pursuing alignment is empowering. Knowing which sacrifices to make prevents us from becoming consumed by our businesses. We begin to proactively make decisions about our time and money without losing focus on our health, relationships, and other important matters. Achieving alignment allows us to live a fulfilled life of purpose. We can be present with the people we care about and the matters that require our attention.

Following these guidelines allays the common feelings of guilt we experience. We don't have to wonder if we're spending too much or too little time on our business. We can achieve business success guilt-free, and our lives and our companies benefit.

MISSION ACCOMPLISHED

When I went on my mission, I thought I was giving up everything for so little. Over time, I realized the sacrifices I made were investments in myself and my future, and the return on those investments was manifold. Even now, over twenty years after returning from my mission in Chile, I lean on lessons and experiences weekly, and sometimes daily, that I wouldn't have had if not for making that "sacrifice." It took a few years for me to gain that perspective, but once I did, I began to see the same pattern play out time and again. As a business owner, it's become a foundation of my success.

The most important choices I make don't come with an instant feedback loop, so I don't expect immediate gratification for my actions. When I spend time with my kids, I don't see them become more confident right away, but I do see it happen over time. When I go to the gym for a workout or play in my weekly pickup basketball game, I might get a shot of endorphins, but the big payoff happens over time, as my stress decreases and my health improves. With every choice, every decision, and every action, I look ahead to the long-term positive effects of the sacrifices I make every day.

Now that you have an understanding of what sacrifices are and how they affect you and your business, it's time to talk about the most common categories and other, more nuanced sacrifices you'll have to make as a business owner. Some of them will surprise you, but knowing what they are will help you prepare so that when they appear, you'll recognize them and know how to respond.

I'm asking you to consider how you use your resources and adjust them. This seems risky, and it is. You don't want to get this part wrong. But as an entrepreneur, you know there's no reward without some risk. But as long as you mitigate the risk with introspection and honesty, identifying your nonnegotiables and committing to protect them, the reward will surely outweigh the risk.

PACK YOUR LUNCH QUESTIONS AND ACTIONS

1. Looking back on your life, what sacrifices did you make that paid off with larger rewards?
2. Which do you value more: security or freedom?
3. What are the things in your life that matter the most?
4. What are some things in your life that you are willing to sacrifice?
5. Make your own list of your life's categories. Prioritize them, identify your nonnegotiables, and come up with your own examples of decisions you've made or may have to make that could impact your categories.

2

YOU MUST BECOME COMFORTABLE WITH RISK

"The biggest risk is not taking any risk... In a world that is changing really quickly, the only strategy that is guaranteed to fail is not taking risks."

—MARK ZUCKERBERG

I grew up in a rural town in Oregon near the border of Idaho. We didn't have a Major League Baseball team in Oregon or Idaho, but we had TBS and WGN. Ted Turner's station aired Atlanta Braves games, and WGN broadcast the Chicago Cubs and White Sox games. If you lived in my town, you were a Braves fan or a Cubs fan, and when my best friend moved to Atlanta when I was five, that sealed my choice.

During the 1990s, the Braves were a dynasty, appearing in the World Series five times that decade. They only won it once—in '95. They lost to the Yankees in 1999 and wouldn't see the World Series again for twenty-two years, in 2021, when they faced the Houston Astros. I had waited so long to see my team make it this far, and I didn't know when it would happen again. Twenty-two years is a long time.

So I flew to Atlanta, bought two tickets for game three, and invited a buddy from high school to join me. We sat in the left field bleachers, which weren't the best seats but weren't bad either, and they were expensive. It was the World Series. The Braves had won the first game in the World Series and lost game two. That night, they made it 2–1. I decided to stay for game four, but my friend had to fly home for work, so I'd be going alone. That's when I got the wild idea to splurge. After all, it was game four of the World Series, and my favorite team was up 2–1! I'd had my eye on the only seat left behind the Braves' dugout. It was going for $7,000 plus all the fees, but no one had picked it up. Being the responsible husband I was (and still am), I called my wife.

"Honey, I'm thinking of buying this ticket…"

She said what any reasonable spouse would say: "Okay, but how are you going to feel if you blow almost $10,000 on a seat and they lose the game?"

Without thinking, I responded, "Not as bad as I'll feel if I don't buy it and they win."

What does this have to do with being a business owner? My wife was looking at our decision from the risk perspective. I could end up spending a lot of money for disappointment and regret. I was looking at it from the reward perspective. I'd be risking the money, but the potential reward was a memory like no other—a memory I could carry with me the rest of my life. The risk of not taking that chance—the opportunity cost—was too high for me to pass up.

Starting a business comes with risk. That risk comes with the potential for rewards, so you have to know what you're risking and what you have to gain if the risk pays off. You shouldn't risk your nonnegotiables, but everything else is up for grabs—but only if the reward is commensurate with or greater than the risk. Walking along the edge of a cliff is extremely risky, and if all you're going to get back is a selfie for Instagram, that's not a risk I'd want to take. Still, you must not be afraid to take risks. As I posted on my Instagram recently, "Stop being afraid of what could go wrong and start being excited about what could go right."

Entrepreneurs have to take risks. It's the only way to receive the reward of being a business owner. The key is to weigh the risk against the potential reward to see if the risk is worth it. Choose your risks carefully, and mitigate the risk by understanding what you may be sacrificing and what you have to gain.

Stop being afraid of what could go wrong and start being excited about what could go right.

Taking risks is emotional. There's uncertainty—will the risk pay off? There's fear—what if it doesn't? You have to learn to weigh risks objectively and not let your emotions get the better of you. Fear comes and goes (and we'll talk about that particular emotion in detail in Chapter 13), but risk is continuous and never-ending because every decision you make and action you take carries a certain amount of it. You can go to the grocery store and risk being run over in the parking lot by a delivery truck, or you can stay home. Staying in the house feels safer, though, right? Even though we'll run out of food eventually and starve to death. Even though our house could get hit by a meteor. Those outcomes seem so far-fetched that we might be inclined to stay home. But we've gone to the store so many times and have never been run over, so we're acclimated to the risk and willing to take it. The risks entrepreneurs take are new, and they can be scary. We have to train ourselves to see them as no different from grocery shopping— necessary to our survival and with the potential for massive rewards.

Once you have a motivation or idea to do something, you can never return to neutral ground. Once a potential action occurs to you ("I should start a business" or "I should turn off the TV and go play at the park with my kids"), it's no longer risk or nothing. It's risk or lost opportunity. And risk is less scary than regret.

My dad had a healthy attitude toward risk. He had a car shop, and he'd buy wrecked vehicles at salvage, fix them up, and sell them. When a customer expressed concern over the salvage title, wondering if a vehicle would actually run, he'd quip, "Well, it was running when it got in a wreck." My father passed away in 2009, but my siblings and I still laugh about the truth of his response.

The uncertainty of risk has a silver lining. You can imagine the outcome if it doesn't pay off, but you can't predict with absolute certainty the best-case scenario if it does. Starting a business could deliver rewards beyond your wildest dreams. Your business could explode. You could become very wealthy. (And if your favorite baseball team makes a comeback after twenty-two years, you could be in a financial position to afford a front-row seat to watch them play in the World Series.)

Risk is less scary than regret.

Again, it comes back to packing your lunch. You have to take the risk of taking the time to pack your lunch instead of the bigger risk of grabbing fast food. The repercussions of that bigger risk aren't felt right away, but they will impact you down the road.

ARE YOU A RISK-TAKER OR RISK-AVOIDER?

Not everyone is cut out to be an entrepreneur. If your risk tolerance is so low that you get physically ill over the idea of risking anything, you might want to consider another career.

Take my mom. Even though she supports my entrepreneurism, she falls squarely at the low-risk end of the spectrum. She not only looks out for her own safety and security, but she also watches over mine. When cryptocurrency dipped, she texted me, asking if I would survive the crypto downturn. I didn't even know what she was talking about and had to google it. Apparently, Bitcoin had dropped significantly that day, which is common because it's a volatile currency. Since I didn't have my life savings invested in it (seriously, far from it), I wasn't actively following crypto news, hadn't noticed the drop, and frankly, wasn't concerned. Mom, on the other hand, was very concerned. I love my mother. She'll never be an entrepreneur, and that's fine. She knows who she is, just as I know who I am and you know who you are. Chances are you're closer to my end of the spectrum than my mom's.

Risks can come at you when you least expect them and catch you totally off guard too. One of my business partners assured me from the start that he had a high tolerance for risk. Yet when he discovered he wasn't going to be rich within six months, his tolerance quickly diminished. He was worried about his finances and unwilling to risk growing the business without a guarantee that he would make a certain income by a certain date. That's not how business works. You can set goals and work toward them. You can achieve them. But there are no guarantees, and that's part of the risk. There's no way around it.

This is one reason so many more people are employees instead of business owners. Risk tolerance separates people like you and me from the majority of people. It doesn't make us better, but it does make us special, and the world needs special people. We are the risk-takers. We are the builders. Imagine if no one had the stomach to start a business. In business you are constantly trying to separate yourself from other people. Taking risks others are unwilling to take creates that separation.

You can't always choose the risk, but you can choose the degree to which you take that risk. That business partner was worried about growing the business, but what if he had set his apprehension aside and approached the problem logically? Instead of taking out a loan for $50,000, what if he took out a loan for $25,000? Would he be comfortable with that risk? Maybe. But he let his emotions get the better of him, and he went back to his day job. The sad thing is that if he had been able to tolerate the risk, he would be a business owner today. And a very wealthy one at that.

I don't expect you to change your risk tolerance. You have yours, I have mine, and neither is superior. It's not about what is right or wrong. I do want you to know and accept that being a business owner requires taking risks—and not just once, but many times throughout the course of your career. You should be comfortable with your choices and not feel pressured. You should not take risks that affect your nonnegotiables. You shouldn't do anything that would have a disastrous impact on your life and from which you could not recover.

Ease into risk. Take them on one at a time, in small bites, to test your tolerance. Figure out how good you are at weighing risks. Figure out how resilient you are—how quickly you recover when a risk doesn't pay off.

RISK AND PARTNERSHIPS

Partners add a new dimension to starting a business. If your risk tolerances don't align, you'll have to compromise over decisions. Your partner might have an overall higher or lower tolerance, or their tolerance will differ from yours over certain things.

I had a business partner who was averse to hiring people even though I believe bringing in staff is necessary to growth. Whenever we started interviewing, he got nervous about the money we'd have to spend on additional salaries, whereas I saw it as a necessary business expense—and a risk we had to take, or we'd risk losing the opportunity to build the business. You might have a partner who's comfortable with risking money on people, but they don't trust investing that same money in marketing. In each instance, it's not about the money, it's about the return on the investment and whether you and they are comfortable with the odds of it paying off.

I've seen risk end the dreams of many entrepreneurs. It has happened within my own businesses enough times that now I recognize the symptoms. A colleague sees what I'm doing and wants to join me on a new venture. They enter that honeymoon phase where everything's exciting and new. Then at the first sign of risk, the rose-colored glasses fall off and they run for the hills. So I've improved my process for vetting new partners, and I emphasize the fact that they must be risk-tolerant or they won't last. Then I prepare for the signs, and when they appear, we have a talk. They must understand that I, and now they, as my partner, have a fiduciary duty to the business. We have a responsibility to our employees and customers. Being a business owner is like being in a marriage—you can't just walk out when it stops being fun.

Having a partner is a risk in itself, and a sacrifice that—if it's the right person for the business—pays off long term. You might not always agree and even have regrets about the partnership from time to time, but you have to see the big picture and how the partnership helps you achieve your top-level goals. If you decide the partnership isn't working for you, you can exit the business or buy out the partner. Each choice comes with risk, so weigh your options carefully before making a decision.

Risks don't always pan out. But they seldom deliver nothing. You at least learn a lesson, like what doesn't work, what not to do next time, or what to do differently. You also learn something about yourself, like how adaptable, resilient, and just plain tough you are. You took a risk, it didn't pay off, and your world didn't end. Hey, look at you. You're a survivor and a thriver. What else can you do? The more risks you take that pay off with big rewards—or fail without ending your world—the more you grow as a person and a business owner.

DETERMINING WHICH RISKS TO TAKE

Risk tolerance comes with experience, and experience shapes your tolerance toward particular risks. When I've hired people in the past, my businesses grew. That doesn't mean it will always work out that way, though, only that I've tested the risk, it paid off, and so I'm willing to take that risk again.

Risks you're willing to take also depend on your top-level goals. If I'm trying to accomplish a big goal, the risk involved seems more reasonable than if I were going after something less important. Going big picture, I can look at my seven life categories and see where the risk falls and how it will impact each category. I avoid risks that could affect my nonnegotiables. I'm open to taking risks that affect my finances and my businesses.

You'll have to take risks throughout your career as a business owner. When confronted with choices, consider whether they could affect your nonnegotiables and the degree of impact they could have. Are you comfortable with that degree of risk?

Then look at the categories your choices will affect directly. I quit a legal career to start a business, and I was happy to take that risk. Once I had a successful company, I took more risks by starting more businesses. That choice aligned with my long-term goal of having a certain number of companies within a certain amount of time. Identifying your top-level, most important goals and your long-term goals can help you make the right choice for yourself. This goes back to the vision board mentioned in Chapter 1. Think about what your life will look like in five, ten, and twenty years and decide if what you are doing now is pointing you in the right direction.

Another way to look at risk is by considering the best and worst potential outcomes. Here's an exercise for you: When you're faced with a risk, take a piece of paper and draw a line down the middle. At the top of the page, write down the risk. It might be "hire a new manager," "take on a partner," or "invest $X in marketing." On the left side of the line, write down all the worst things that could happen if that risk doesn't work out. On the right side, write down everything good that could happen if it does.

Putting it on paper will help you see the worst-case possibilities, and there's a good chance they're not as bad as you think. Then again, maybe they are, but at least now you know what they really are, and your imagination isn't running wild and turning your emotions upside down. Writing down the best outcome explores possibilities you haven't considered because you've been busy worrying about those worst-case scenarios. It's common for negative outcomes to come to us more readily, while the possible good outcomes remain more hidden.

I do some hard-money lending, which is lending private companies—which may not qualify for traditional (bank) loans—money at higher interest rates. The worst outcome for me is not getting paid back. So I consider what that means: If I don't get paid back, will I go out of business? Will I lose my home? Will the loss impact my lifestyle? Affect my belief in God? Cause harm to my family and my health? The answer to all those questions is no. On the other hand, if I am paid back, what do I gain? Well, I'll get all my money back plus 35 percent interest, which is more than I'd make in a traditional investment.

Imagining worst- and best-case scenarios takes the emotion out of your decisions. The fear, anxiety, and uncertainty are put to rest so you can be free to make a logical decision based on your situation. When you approach risk this way, you might find that you have a higher tolerance than you thought.

WELCOME OPPORTUNITIES, AVOID REGRETS

By reframing what we see as sacrifices, we see the benefit of making small sacrifices for something much greater. This is the epitome of risk analysis. We look at what we are giving up and what it could deliver in return. We also consider the risk of not taking the risk—the lost opportunity. Even though taking a risk can cause short-term challenges, making that choice can deliver grand results long term, helping us meet major goals.

When you don't take a risk, you accept the opportunity cost. So when you don't start a business because you can't accept the risk, you accept the risk of regretting that decision for the rest of your life. If you're like me, you'll be sitting at your desk in some job you don't love, daydreaming about that business you could have had. You will forever live with a voice in your head asking, "What if?"

Nothing great was ever accomplished without significant risks. As you begin the process of starting your business, prepare to take risks. Welcome them for the opportunities they make possible.

Risk-takers have made a name for themselves in the business world. We don't often hear about the risks that didn't pay off, but those that did are legendary.

- **Elon Musk**—Co-founder of PayPal, Tesla, SpaceX, Neuralink, and the Boring Company. Musk took significant financial risks, especially with Tesla and SpaceX, investing his own money when both companies faced potential bankruptcy.
- **Steve Jobs**—Co-founder of Apple Inc. Jobs took several risks throughout his career, including the development of the Macintosh and the iPhone, both of which revolutionized their respective markets.
- **Jeff Bezos**—Founder of Amazon. Bezos left a stable job in finance to start an online bookstore, which he expanded into the world's largest online retailer.
- **Mark Zuckerberg**—Co-founder of Facebook. Zuckerberg dropped out of Harvard to focus on building Facebook, which has since become one of the most influential social media platforms in the world.
- **Richard Branson**—Founder of the Virgin Group. Branson has started numerous businesses in diverse industries, from music to airlines, often taking bold risks to enter and disrupt new markets.
- **Sara Blakely**—Founder of Spanx. Blakely invested her life savings into developing her idea for footless pantyhose, which turned into a billion-dollar shapewear company.
- **Reed Hastings**—Co-founder of Netflix. Hastings took a major risk by transitioning Netflix from a DVD rental service to a streaming

platform, a move that ultimately transformed the entertainment industry.

- **Howard Schultz**—Former CEO of Starbucks. Schultz risked his career and finances to purchase Starbucks and transform it from a small Seattle coffee chain into a global brand.
- **Jack Ma**—Co-founder of Alibaba Group. Ma took a huge risk in launching an e-commerce business in China when internet usage was still in its infancy in the country.
- **Larry Page and Sergey Brin**—Co-founders of Google. They took a risk in leaving their PhD programs to develop their search engine, which has become the foundation of one of the most powerful technology companies in the world.
- **Tony Hsieh**—Zappos tech multimillionaire and author of Delivering Happiness. Hsieh invested all of his money into his business, which was a huge risk. Hsieh's customer service policies, such as return policies, were adopted by companies like Amazon. Hsieh revolutionized online sales by allowing people to return shoes at no cost, which wasn't heard of at the time. That policy removed the risk of being stuck with shoes that didn't fit for customers.

Risk is a means to an end. Learn to analyze it objectively. Leverage it as a tool to achieve your goals. Taking risks is necessary to becoming a successful business owner, and your ability to manage it sets you apart from people who will never be where you are, doing what you are doing. When you encounter risk, get excited. See it as an opportunity to accomplish something great. Changing your relationship with risk empowers you to make decisions that propel you toward entrepreneurial success. Risk equals opportunity for you and the possibility for reward. It separates you from the pack.

BE BRAVE

Remember that Braves game? When I bought the ticket, I didn't know if they'd win. But viewing the risk objectively and accepting the best-case and worst-case scenarios empowered me to make the right decision. Weighing the risk of buying the ticket to see my team lose against the regret of not buying it and missing a potential win made my choice simple. I would have been happy whether they won or lost the game, and the experience made the cost worth every penny. I sat behind the dugout at a Braves game during the World Series!

The game was fantastic. Incredible. The Braves won. *They won!* Afterward was a blur, but I remember hugging a lot of complete strangers. I was tempted to stay for game five, but it was Halloween, and I wanted to get home to take my kids trick-or-treating. Some things are more important than your favorite team making the World Series (remember your priority list). The Braves lost the game on Halloween anyway, but they won the World Series with the next game, in Houston.

Taking the risk to buy that ticket gave me a memory I will cherish for the rest of my life. And what's more, I don't know when the Braves will ever be back in the World Series. And the same is true for you. When is another opportunity going to come along that you currently have in front of you? The opportunity to start and run the business of your dreams is precious. If you're up for the risk, don't let it slip away.

PACK YOUR LUNCH QUESTIONS AND ACTIONS

1. On a scale from 1 to 10, 10 being the biggest risk-taker, how would you rate yourself?
2. What is the riskiest financial move you have ever made?
3. Do you feel like being risk averse is holding you back from achieving your goals?
4. Do you believe that risks are ever as scary as we first believe them to be?

3

YOU WILL HAVE TO SACRIFICE FINANCIAL SECURITY

"Chase the vision, not the money; the money will end up following you."

—TONY HSIEH

The novice entrepreneur thinks starting a business will make them instantly rich. It's no wonder they have that impression. Skim the social media posts of some business owners and you'd think they all drove Lambos and spent their days drinking champagne and cruising around on their yachts!

No doubt the financial possibilities are endless. But let's set the record straight. Getting rich is not guaranteed, and it never happens overnight.

I remember sitting in my office at my last legal job. I was frustrated, working on a project I was struggling to care about, when one of the partners walked in and asked me to do something else. I had to do it. My paycheck depended on it. In that moment, I thought, "When I have my own business, I'll have complete control over my time and money. I'll be rich enough to pass this kind of work on to someone else!"

Fast-forward three months. Now I'm a business owner, and things haven't turned out the way I imagined. In one day, I'm trying to interview a potential new hire, answer customer service calls, order products, and pay my vendors. I'm looking at the time and wondering when I'll be able to get out of here. But I can't leave. My business depends on it. In the middle of all this, I have a fleeting memory of that moment in the legal office where I imagined how different life would be as a business owner. My next thought is "What the hell was I thinking?"

I thought being a business owner would give me more control over my time and money. And it did—but not right away. That took years and a lot of experience figuring out how to manage the differences between being an employ*ee* and an employ*er*. As an employee, I had a boss or two and a direct report. As an employer, I was answering to employees, customers, vendors, and partners. There were hundreds of people making demands on my time, and time is money. The more time I spent answering to all my new "bosses," the less time I had to figure out ways to improve my business so it would make more money. What a difference from the "good old days" when I didn't have to think about my paycheck—those days when, every week like clockwork, a certain amount of money appeared in my bank account, like magic!

As a business owner, I had to keep a close eye on my finances and make adjustments. For the first year and a half, I lived off savings and paid myself just $24,000 a year from my business profits. I could have let that temporary hit to my finances throw me off track. But I reminded myself not only of what I had given up but what I had gained. I may have lost my financial security—at least for a couple of years—but I was going after my dreams. And I knew that if I could survive this initial, difficult period, I would eventually gain the control and flexibility I dreamed of.

Starting a business doesn't come with financial security, not at first, and if you don't make the right sacrifices, maybe never. But if you make the right sacrifices in the short term, you will pave the way to financial freedom in the long term.

I didn't understand that right away. Over time, I learned that to be paid for more than you do, you first must do more than you are paid for. For me, financial freedom happened around four or five years into my entrepreneurial career. *To be paid more for what I did, I first had to do more than I was paid for.* And when I was finally paid more for my work, I was also making money for doing no work at all, thanks to the economies of scale and being able to repurpose all the lessons I'd learned and processes I'd developed at the start of my career. So I could do less, make more, and also bring in passive income.

> To be paid for more than you do, you first must do more than you are paid for.

IN BUSINESS, THERE ARE NO OVERNIGHT SUCCESSES

New business owners are prone to spending money they don't have. They see jet-setting entrepreneurs bragging about their lavish lifestyles on social media and get the impression that wealth happens overnight. I wish those jet-setters would include details with their posts, like how many years they worked and sacrifices they made to get where they are today. A little transparency, people?

I deal with these misconceptions in my own business. One of my newer businesses is just getting off the ground, and I'm excited about its prospects. But today it's not making any money. Becoming profitable takes time. So for now, it's operating from a line of credit that I extended to it, which is how I launch many startups. And like those other startups, I hired an operational partner to run the business. When I hire an operational partner, I make it clear that the business is their 100 percent full-time job. It's their eight-to-five and then some, their everyday responsibility. The business will not survive without their undivided attention. They should plan to take on that role for an agreed-upon salary for the first few years, and then, depending on the business, we can talk about increasing their pay.

Most of my partners understand why this approach is necessary. But every once in a while, they miss the point. Recently, one of my operational partners messaged me. He was starting another business on the side, he said, but he didn't want me to worry because he'd stay on top of all his duties with our business. I appreciated him telling me what he was up to, but I was dismayed that he thought he'd have time to spare. I've started enough companies to know how much time and focus each new one requires, and starting a second one before the first one is profitable is a recipe for disaster. At just one year into the startup, he was not in a position to start a second company.

I thought about why he might think he could run another business so soon. Part of the reason may have been because he was surrounded by other people like me who ran multiple businesses. Maybe he didn't realize we had started them one by one and not all at once, and not until each one was operating without my day-to-day involvement.

But he's a smart guy. So why the desire to take this risk? It was not a small sacrifice, but a major one that could affect his ability to succeed in the business we shared. I pressed him for details and got my answer. He needed more money. The salary we had agreed on wasn't cutting it, he said. Again, I wondered where the miscommunication had occurred. He knew the salary going into the job. Well, it turned out that right after becoming my operational partner, he had bought a new house and a lot of other things he couldn't afford. He was living like a $250,000 a year entrepreneur instead of an $80,000 a year entrepreneur with his first startup. By the way, he had started at $60,000, and I had increased his salary another $20,000 that year, partly out of goodwill and partly because he was working hard and I could see the company thriving under his management. But now he needed money to pay for all those things he thought he should have, not to mention all the other things his wife was pressuring him to buy.

I've seen one company after another tank because the owners relied on profits too soon to fund lifestyles that outpaced company growth. Startups do not have money. They rely on investments—borrowed money—to get off the ground. Most startups don't launch in Silicon Valley with $10 million in seed funding and a $500,000 paycheck for the CEO. A small percentage of businesses start that way, and many of them fail.

Expect to make less money as a business owner than you made as an employee, at first. Not forever. But if you start off by spending more than you make, you will never make more than you are worth, and you'll be right back where you started—getting paid for every hour of work you put in, no more, no less.

> Expect to make less money as a business owner than you made as an employee, at first.

A dollar to a startup company is worth a hundred dollars to a company that's five years down the road. You need to be watching how much comes in and putting it where it can do the most good for the business, not for your personal enjoyment. When I started my pest control company, Proof, I owned three pieces of real estate, single-family three- and four-bedroom homes. I moved my family—myself, my wife, our two children, and my brother—into a two-bedroom apartment and leased all three houses to save money. The passive income from those leases went toward the mortgages with a little left over to help pay for the apartment. I didn't run out and buy a big new house or a fancy car (though all that came later). I didn't take my family on extravagant vacations. We all understood the sacrifices that were necessary and were willing to make them, knowing they would pay off after a few years.

That's exactly what happened. I went from $24,000 (plus my savings) in year one, to $36,000 in year two, to $48,000 in year three, and $500,000+ in year four. I was lucky to have a family that believed in me and was willing to live within our means because the financial security we now enjoy would not have been possible otherwise.

Understand and accept that you will start out making less than you are worth. That concept is tough to accept because entrepreneurs are usually very good at the technical aspect of their job—that product or service they're delivering. It's a blow to your ego to think, "I'm starting a business doing X because I know it inside and out, yet I'm going to make less money than if I did it for some other company."

From plumbers, to electricians, to software engineers—they all make good money working for somebody else. So when they start a plumbing, electrical, or software company, they expect to make a lot more. That's not how it works, because they have to put in the time to build their business before they can meet and eventually exceed their former salary.

Taking a high salary stresses the company. Your business needs that money to operate, upgrade, and scale. The longer you can survive on a small salary, the faster your company will grow and the better the chances it will succeed.

FREEDOM OVER FINANCIAL SECURITY

If starting a business doesn't guarantee financial security, why do it? This is a good time to consider why you want to be an entrepreneur. Financial security is not a valid reason. Instead, you are working for freedom. The freedom, if you put in the time and effort, to make even more money and become financially independent so you can work when you want, how much you want, doing what you want. But first you have to make sacrifices. Then you can achieve not only security, but significant financial prosperity.

By the way, the financial security afforded by working for someone else isn't guaranteed either. Sure, some people stay in the same job for twenty, thirty, even forty years. But companies go bankrupt. They get bought out. They relocate. Employees get laid off. The funny thing is that not everyone sees it that way, especially banks.

A few years ago, one of my employees was getting a home loan at the same time I was, and through the same bank. I had to fill out some paperwork verifying she worked for me, and she got the loan, no problem. The same underwriter gave me a hassle over my paperwork. They said that since I was a business owner, my income wasn't as secure as someone's that was verifiable by an employer. What? This made no sense to me because if my company went under, that employee would have lost her income before I did. Still, this is something to be aware of as an entrepreneur. Other people's financial decisions aren't always logical.

No matter how you earn your money, working for yourself or someone else, it's always a gamble. Whether you bet on someone else's company or bet on yourself is up to you. As long as you make the sacrifice of packing your own lunch—making that minor sacrifice up front—you will come out ahead financially every time.

A LOGICAL APPROACH TO FINANCIAL INDEPENDENCE

The Kauffman Foundation notes that many entrepreneurs had substantial work experience before starting their businesses. According to its report, *The Anatomy of an Entrepreneur*, the average age of first-time entrepreneurs was found to be around forty, and many of them held mid- to senior-level positions before starting their ventures. Salaries in these positions often ranged from $60,000 to $150,000 annually, depending on the industry and role.[3]

As a new business owner, you can't rely on the business to support

---

[3] "The Anatomy of an Entrepreneur," Ewing Marion Kauffman Foundation, July 8, 2009, https://www.kauffman.org/reports/the-anatomy-of-an-entrepreneur/.

you. It may not turn a profit right away and could be operating in the red for a while. When the business does become profitable, you'll need to reinvest that revenue into marketing and growth. So you'll have to adjust your lifestyle and expenses to adapt, living off savings and a small salary. With less income, you'll feel less financially secure.

If you do take a small salary from the business, you still can't count on it. You're not working for a Fortune 500 company anymore, and there is no guarantee that the profit you see one week will continue in the weeks ahead. On top of that, you'll be paying for all your own benefits—health insurance, retirement savings, income tax, and whatever else your old employer was covering from your old salary. For these reasons, you should have at least several months' salary set aside to cover all your living expenses while you are getting the business off the ground. During this time, you may be able to draw a small salary from the startup, but nothing substantial. This fact is hard for entrepreneurs to swallow. Putting aside an entire year's salary is tough. A working spouse can ease the burden, and they may even be able to put you on their insurance, but you still have to plan for no new income for at least a year.

Some entrepreneurs work around this by choosing not to scale their businesses. They don't want to run a company with employees. They're happy to be solopreneurs, which, when you think about it, is like creating a job for yourself and not an actual business. Without staff, it's hard to grow because you are doing all the work. Your income is still tied directly to your time and the hours of work you put in. There's nothing wrong with that choice, and many people prefer the benefits of solopreneurship. Just be aware that choosing that path limits business growth. You can only work so many hours a day.

Some entrepreneurs sidestep the need to have a year's salary set aside by starting their business as a "side hustle." They keep their full-time job and launch a startup in their spare time. While I don't recommend this model, I understand why, for some people, it's the only choice. If you're the sole breadwinner in your family, you have people depending on you for food and shelter, and you aren't earning enough money in your job to save for your first startup year, a side hustle may be the only option.

The problem with the side hustle is you are doing two jobs partway and not giving all your time and attention to just one, which you *should* be doing at your regular job and *have* to do at your startup to get it off the ground quickly. If you're thinking of going in this direction, consider taking on a second, part-time job for a while and putting that extra money aside. Then, when you have enough saved to live on for a year or more, quit your full-time job and launch your business. That way, you'll be able to commit 100 percent of your time and attention to the startup. You'll be less stressed physically, emotionally, and financially with those finances in place and without having to worry about that other job.

However, if starting a business as a side hustle is your only option, go for it. You'll never know how it will turn out if you don't try. It will be harder and take longer, but success is possible. If you don't try, it's not possible at all. Just remember that starting a business comes with sacrifices. However you choose to do it, you'll be sacrificing something. Be aware of your nonnegotiables and protect them.

MINOR SACRIFICES FOR A CHANCE
AT MAJOR RETURNS

Building a business removes your financial "ceiling." You forfeit the steady paycheck temporarily for the opportunity to make much more money than you ever could working for someone else.

I ran a poll on my social media, asking followers if they preferred security or freedom. Nearly everyone responded with "freedom." We all want to believe that's true for ourselves, but when it comes to making the decision to give up a regular paycheck, the choice isn't so easy. This is why many people forfeit their entrepreneurial dreams to remain employees. According to 2016 data from the US Bureau of Labor Statistics and other sources, the US workforce is predominantly composed of employees, who make up approximately 47 percent of the total population, while business owners, despite owning over thirty-one million small businesses, represent only about 10 to 12 percent of the adult population, highlighting the significant disparity in workforce composition in the United States.[4] In 2023, the percentage of employees had risen to 64.2 percent.[5]

During my first month as a business owner, I logged in to my bank account daily and watched my savings slowly being depleted. I wasn't thinking about freedom then—I was starting to freak out. More money was going out than coming in, and I wasn't used to that. It was scary!

Keep in mind that I was married with children. I had serious financial obligations. At the risk of sounding old, I realize that today's young entrepreneurs, fresh out of school and often living at home, don't have those responsibilities. For them, choosing freedom over security doesn't carry the same weight. But for the rest of us, this is a serious choice. We have to be prepared to accept drastic changes to our lifestyles, like moving our families out of our four-bedroom house and into a two-bedroom apartment.

Making that choice separates entrepreneurs from everyone else. Consider the number of business owners compared to employees in the United States. The difference is staggering, and for good reason. It takes guts to start a business. It takes confidence to believe in yourself so much that you're willing to sacrifice financial stability on the outcome. It takes hard work to stick it out long enough to be rewarded with the big payoff. And it takes fortitude to do all of this knowing there are no guarantees. But you were built for this. You got this.

I don't want to come off as a know-it-all. Seriously, I had no idea what I was getting into at first. To give you an idea of my mentality,

---

4   Steven F. Hipple and Laurel A. Hammond, "Self-Employment in the United States," U.S. Bureau of Labor Statistics, March 2016, https://www.bls.gov/spotlight/2016/self-employment-in-the-united-states/pdf/self-employment-in-the-united-states.pdf.

5   U.S. Department of Labor, "Work Experience of the Population—2023," U.S. Bureau of Labor Statistics, December 18, 2024, https://www.bls.gov/news.release/pdf/work.pdf. It is helpful to note that only 70 percent of adult Americans work full time.

let's look at the person I was, even as a young kid. Back in fifth grade, living in a farming community, my teacher assigned each student a plastic Solo cup and a chunk of potato. We had to water it every day. The point was to see how our regular attention to the potato chunk paid off over time. We would be rewarded with a sprout, which would, of course, grow into a potato plant and more potatoes. All we had to do was add water. Well, I watered it the first day, the second day, and so forth. Nothing seemed to be happening, so I quit watering it. There was no immediate gratification. *No fast food.* Why keep watering this stupid cup if I wasn't getting anything in return?

That was an important lesson for me, and though I carried it into my business, I still wasn't prepared for the hardships making less money would cause. But my family stuck by me. So I kept reinvesting almost all the profits from the business into infrastructure, systems, processes, marketing, sales, and personnel. I kept watering that potato until it sprouted. And grow it did. That business not only grew; it flourished.

I invested in different things at different times. First came the marketing and sales to bring in customers, then staff to help take care of the customers. Infrastructure, systems, processes, and training developed over time. My investments became cyclical because the more I built out the company, the more customers I could support, so the more marketing and sales I needed, and so on.

We Americans, and probably most people in first-world countries, compare our lifestyles to those of the people around us. We don't need the best house on the street or fanciest car in the garage, but we don't want the worst ones either. Learn to think outside your neighborhood and community. If you're in the middle class in the US, you have more than most people in the world. Do you have access to healthcare? To healthy foods? Clean water? Do you have air conditioning? A cell phone? More streaming TV channels than you could watch in a lifetime? When it comes down to it, you're doing pretty well in the big scheme of things. You don't want to go backward and give up any of those things. But maybe you could give up something. Take a look at your bank statement and see where the money's going. Look for places to cut back. You can probably give up more than you think without seriously affecting your quality of life. Do you really need that six-dollar cup of coffee every day?

As I mentioned earlier, spending money you don't have is a sure way to sink your business. I've had many partners over the years—those who were willing to make financial sacrifices in the short term went on to build thriving companies. The ones who got themselves into debt with new houses, cars, and family vacations struggled and eventually gave up and went back to their old jobs.

When I meet with a new potential partner, we always have this conversation. No one—I mean no one—wants to hear it. I'm telling them that they won't make more money right away. They will make less than they're used to. And they're going to have to work harder for it. No matter how clearly I think I'm communicating this message, some get it and others don't. The ones who do sit down with their families, their credit card statements, and their bank statements. They visit every expense, every subscription, and every membership. Then they start cutting. They do the hard work that comes before the hard work of running a business. Others, well, they go shopping. You can imagine how that turns out.

By the way, your life will not change that much if you cancel half your streaming subscriptions. You won't be less happy. But if you put that money toward marketing that brings in customers, you'll be that much further along in your quest for financial freedom.

(THE THINGS YOU BUY WITH) MONEY CAN'T BUY HAPPINESS

When I started making good money—enough to bump up my salary—I relaxed my budget. In time, I began spending money on all those things I thought would make me happy. Yes, I bought Ferraris. I really like my Ferrari, but to my surprise, owning them has not been a life-altering experience. You know what makes me happy? More time with my family. Putting food on the table. Knowing my kids won't have to struggle as much as I did (though I sometimes wonder if I'll come to regret how much easier they'll have it). Knowing my wife sleeps better, not worrying about her financial future. So while having more money makes me happy, the material things I buy with it—all those cool toys I thought would make me a happier person—have turned out to be fun in the short term, but over time, they're not such a big deal. Like Dr. Robert Waldinger, a psychiatrist at Harvard, notes, "Life happiness is not a quick fix—it is the hard work of tending to your closest relationships."[6]

Are you looking forward to owning a private jet? I hear that a lot from entrepreneurs. They can't wait to have that jet, as if it's proof of success. I ask myself, "How exactly is that jet going to bring them happiness? Where are they traveling so often that they need their own high-speed airborne transportation?" Most business is done online and over the phone. Granted, standing in front of your own jet makes for a very cool Instagram post, but after all the likes and the comments, what do you have to show for that investment? I mean, other than a monthly jet payment, storage payment, and higher insurance?

But if you want a jet, and your business is making so much money that you can afford one, then by all means—get yourself a jet. Just don't expect instant happiness. Something to consider when you're getting ready to pull the trigger on that next big purchase.

DRAPER'S FINANCIAL HIERARCHY OF NEEDS

It's likely you've heard of Maslow's Hierarchy of Needs, a triangular diagram where the base of the triangle represents a person's basic physiological needs such as food and water, and subsequent layers represent safety and so forth, culminating in the top layer, self-actualization. I developed a similar hierarchy for business owners

---

6   Parker Houston, "Lessons in Happiness from 75 Years of Harvard Research," Leadyoufirst, July 2022, https:// leadyoufirst.com/lessons-in-happiness-from-75-years-of-research-at-harvard/.

and their finances. It applies to people in general, but especially entre-preneurs because there's no ceiling to how much money they can make. Maslow's Hierarchy starts with a foundation of the basics of survival. Draper's Financial Hierarchy of Needs is similar but focused on financial needs, and while there may be some variation about the specifics from person to person, this is generally how individuals progress financially throughout their lifetime. Some spend longer in certain categories, while others may skip a category (status, for example) altogether. Each layer of the hierarchy includes what matters to you, and some may be more complete than others, but each one should include something.

SURVIVAL

My survival foundation includes not simply food, but healthy food. Since I live in Phoenix, where we have very hot summers, my shelter has to include great air conditioning. This category is all about earning sufficient income to provide the minimum for survival.

STATUS

You may be seeking approval from your peers, colleagues, or family members, so your status may include "own a private jet" or simply "my teacher who always said I would never amount to anything sees that I have a successful business and a wonderful family." Or you may be chasing status for professional reasons, perhaps to be seen as a thought leader or to bring in clients and generate business. Status is more critical to the entrepreneur trying to build their podcast subscriber list than to a business owner who prefers to stay out of the spotlight. Consider the reason behind your desired status.

A rule of thumb here is to consider how much time you spend in front of customers. When I was a practicing attorney, status was very important because I couldn't meet with clients looking as if I had just crawled out of bed. I had to convey an appearance of prosperity and professionalism. Humans judge each other quickly as a survival mechanism. We want to know whom to trust, and status helps us gain the trust of others quickly. Status can be tricky, though. Depending on your motivation, it can make other people feel badly about themselves. It can be leveraged to influence people to do things that aren't in their best interests. Think about why status is important to you and what you plan to do with it.

Some entrepreneurs aren't comfortable advertising their knowledge and success, which is critical to building status. If your goals depend on it, you have to step outside your comfort zone. This is why the reason is so important. If your goals don't depend on status and you don't want to promote yourself, then status could be of minor importance to you. I know very successful entrepreneurs who have no interest at all in elevating their status. It's a personal decision that only you can make.

FREEDOM

Freedom to me is control over my time. It's doing what I want, when I want, with whom I want to do it. Freedom is possible when you have the infrastructure and people in place that allow you to step aside and remove yourself from the day-to-day operations. You have enough money coming in to live the life you want to live, and how you spend your time doesn't affect that money flow.

Before you get to freedom, time and money are constrained and possibly causing you pain. Freedom is a great thing to have, and getting to it is a terrific place to be, but it is not the "be-all and end-all" many people expect. It's just a new stage. Once you are there, you need to find purpose beyond building your business and attaining freedom. Otherwise, why get out of bed?

Identify what freedom means to you. Define it in stages. If freedom for you revolves around money and time, how much is enough? Working twenty hours a week and taking your family on three vacations a year? Not working at all, and just being available for emergencies?

Take a look at your life's categories to remind yourself what matters. Your freedom should involve those initial categories—the nonnegotiables. Make sure you are working toward attaining time, money, and other resources to be free to satisfy those categories ahead of the others.

When I was a kid, I ate cheap store-brand cereal for breakfast. My parents couldn't afford the name brands. So I watched those TV commercials with the leprechaun, the rainbow, and the pot of gold, and I wondered what all that magically delicious talk was about. Those marshmallow bits sure looked better than what was in my cereal bowl! So I raked leaves, made a few bucks, and immediately rode my bike to the only grocery store in town with only one mission: buy a box of Lucky Charms. I ate the entire box of cereal, and when I took that last bite, I was done with Lucky Charms. My desire was satisfied. I had attained cereal freedom, and the last thing I wanted was another box of cereal. I immediately started thinking about what else I could get if I raked more leaves. Once you get to your highest level of freedom, what will you do next?

LEGACY

Entrepreneurs who achieve their version of freedom move on to build legacies. They want to impact the people around them during their lifetime in a way that ensures their impact will continue after they're gone. They also want to be remembered for something other than being great businesspeople. Entrepreneurs build legacies by putting their time and money behind other projects that will outlive them. They start foundations and charities, or they build organizations that align with their values.

Everyone leaves a legacy. Some are just much more proactive about it. Some people just want to run their businesses and not worry about whether they have a lasting impact. Others prefer to step away from their companies and simply retire from work and the public eye. For legacy builders, the work they do beyond achieving that state of freedom is intertwined with their legacy. Their work becomes their legacy, and their legacy, their work.

Bill Gates, Elon Musk, and Warren Buffett have legacies. Buffett has a pact with other extremely wealthy individuals called "die with nothing," where they all agree to give away all their money before they die.[7] I believe that our goal should *not* be to live forever but to create something that *does*.

THE TEN LAWS THAT GOVERN MONEY

Making financial sacrifices early in your business can deliver high-value rewards in the future. These sacrifices are possible when you understand the ten laws that govern money.

I have spent the last twenty years reading books about building wealth. From these books, I have come to believe that there are laws that govern wealth, just like there are laws that govern the physical world (e.g., the law of gravity). When we follow these laws, wealth is sure to follow. Over the years, I have compiled these central laws, distilled from numerous financial books:

1. **To accumulate wealth, you must first believe you are worthy of it.** Imposter syndrome and other insecurities lead to you feeling as if you don't deserve to be wealthy. As you build and grow your business, you'll grow as a person and eventually realize that you deserve the money. You do. You earned it.
2. **You must give away at least 10 percent of everything you make.**
3. **You must save at least 10 percent of everything you make.** You can invest it, but you cannot spend it.
4. **You must increase your ability to earn by creating passive income so your investments work for you.**
5. **You must diversify your assets with a mix of high-risk/**

---

7   Warren Buffett, "My Philanthropic Pledge," The Giving Pledge, accessed February 4, 2025, https://givingpledge.org/pledger?pledgerId=177.

high-reward, medium-risk/medium-reward, and low-risk/low-reward investments.

6. **You must buy low and sell high.** As Warren Buffett put it, "[We] simply attempt to be fearful when others are greedy and [to be] greedy only when others are fearful."[8]
7. **You must have multiple streams of income.**
8. **You must take risks.**
9. **You must use debt wisely to achieve incremental growth.**
10. **You must put off short-term satisfaction in exchange for long-term growth (i.e., pack your lunch).**

PACK YOUR LUNCH, AND MONEY—AND FREEDOM—WILL FOLLOW

When starting a business, expect to make less money than you made at the job you left. Make that sacrifice and, over time, you'll make more money than you would have if you had stayed in the job. It's the only way to get out from under an employer's rules around how much you're worth. Think of being a business owner as investing in yourself. As you get more experience in your new role, your value increases. Like compounding interest, your time and effort generates more income over time.

You might think you're not a good investment, but don't let imposter syndrome derail your plans. Imposter syndrome creates fear and anxiety that worsens when it's applied to financial security. If you can't make a go of this business idea, how will you eat? Where will you live? That's why it's important to get a handle on it early. Prepare financially. Have a year's salary or more set aside before quitting your job. Cut your expenses. And when that voice in your head casts doubt on your abilities, tell it where to go. Remind that voice that you've thought ahead, made a plan, and are making the sacrifices required to

---

8   Warren Buffett, "Letter to the Shareholders of Berkshire Hathaway Inc.," Berkshire Hathaway, accessed February 4, 2025, https://www.berkshirehathaway.com/letters/1986.html.

succeed. Tell that voice to come back later, in a few years, and you'll show it what's possible when you believe in yourself. You are worth taking a chance on, and if you put in the effort and make the sacrifices, you will live up to your expectations. Believe in yourself.

Learn and practice the laws that govern wealth. They are time-tested rules of thumb that lead to prosperity, and as a business owner, financial freedom is only possible if you are responsible with your money.

Instead of seeing sacrifices as negatives, see them as positives—tools at your disposal for launching and scaling your business more quickly and successfully. They are the hidden opportunities many entrepreneurs overlook and avoid. Leverage them to be among the business owners who achieve their goals. Make these short-term financial sacrifices to achieve financial freedom and eventually create your own legacy. This mindset shift will change your attitude toward sacrifices. You won't dread them. You'll get excited about them and the possibilities they allow.

When I started my business, I thought I'd have more money and more time. Boy, was I wrong. But I didn't give up, and in time, my short-term sacrifices paid off with more control over my resources. My life isn't perfect, and I still have very busy days when I don't spend as much time as I'd like with my family. But it's gotten much better, and with each day that passes, I'm able to apply my resources toward those things that matter most—my nonnegotiables.

PACK YOUR LUNCH QUESTIONS AND ACTIONS

1. Do you value freedom or security more?
2. If you had to cut how much you spend in half for two years, could you do it?
3. Have you ever had to live off less than you make?
4. What is your financial plan for starting or growing your business?

4

YOU WILL HAVE LESS TIME FOR HOBBIES

"Don't be afraid to give up the good to go for the great."

—JOHN D. ROCKEFELLER

Moving from Phoenix to Michigan, I left my social life behind. I had gone to law school at Arizona State and become close with my classmates. Practicing law, I got to know my colleagues. Those were the people with whom I shared my hobbies and pastimes. Moving away from them meant moving away from all the activities that made me happy outside of home and work. No more going out with the guys (by the way, being a nondrinker meant I was always the designated driver, a role I gladly accepted). No more basketball with the guys. No more anything besides running my business and tending to my nonnegotiables. This was a sacrifice I would have to make for two to three years as a new business owner. Not only did I find some workarounds, but I also discovered better ways to spend my time.

I realized some of my hobbies were essential to my physical and mental health, so I had to either hang on to them or swap them out for something that took less time but delivered the same results. One of the first things to go was golf. Between the commute, playing, and lunch afterward, I was spending six hours per round of golf. I didn't realize my time commitment to the sport had become the equivalent of a part-time job. Giving up golf—or at least cutting back—didn't ruin my life, though. I started going to the gym, which took a fifth of the time. That new hobby helped me get into the best shape of my life (and saved my mental health). I discovered other workarounds too.

Some of my favorite pastimes turned out to be activities that my children also enjoyed. Surprisingly, one of my kids decided he liked playing golf. Suddenly, I was back on the golf course. In addition to the physical and mental benefits, golf also became family time, satisfying another of my nonnegotiables. I hung on to the hobbies that relieved stress, kept me healthy, and satisfied more than a single nonnegotiable, and I abandoned the rest.

INTENTIONAL SACRIFICES, FEWER REGRETS

You don't have to give up everything, but you will have to make some sacrifices. Sometimes that means doing something less frequently or swapping it out for something similar that takes less time or can be combined with another essential area of your life. Hang on to hobbies and habits that satisfy your nonnegotiables, such as meditation, hiking, going to the gym, basketball, and other physical and mental activities. They might eat up an hour of time but can add years to your life. Look for ways to combine them, and other hobbies, with your nonnegotiables.

If you give up everything you love about life, you'll begin to regret your business. That's not a good position to be in. You should be excited about your business and look forward to working in it and on it, not dreading it. On the other hand, the only way you'll have enough time to run it is by sacrificing hobbies that don't move it forward or contribute to your nonnegotiables.

Owning a business demands becoming more deliberate with your time. You have to be more efficient, at least until you've reached a state of freedom where your business can operate without you. (First you do what you have to do, then you do what you're good at, and then you do what you want to do.) In the meantime, you need to work enough, be intentional about your time, and also make sure not to burn out. This can be difficult in a culture that glorifies work. But without time to relax and recover, our physical and mental capabilities decline and we can't be the people our businesses need to survive.

Owning a business demands becoming more deliberate with your time.

We're all familiar with the stories of entrepreneurs who sacrificed everything. "I'll sleep when I'm dead," they say, and that statement becomes a self-fulfilling prophecy. They never get to enjoy life, they suffer with health and family problems, and they die years before their time is up.

Larry Miller, for example, who started one of the largest automobile dealerships in the United States and became the owner of the NBA franchise Utah Jazz, worked around the clock. In his biography, he claims that he didn't have time to care for his health. Miller ate fast food. He didn't exercise. He had diabetes, which led to amputations. And he died in 2009 at the age of sixty-four.[9] By saving thirty minutes here and there, he eventually took years, possibly decades, off of his life. He quite literally failed to pack his lunch and chose fast food instead.

It's easy to fall into that kind of lifestyle. You'll think, "Oh, I'll skip a healthy lunch this one time and grab a burger and fries later" or "I'll skip the gym just this one day," but those one times and one days

---

9   Larry H. Miller and Doug Robinson, *Driven: An Autobiography* (Shadow Mountain, 2010).

become a new habit, and before you know it, you're in rough shape. We justify the behavior by telling ourselves that being a workaholic is a good thing to be worn proudly like a badge of honor. We brag about how many hours we put in every day, every week. But if we ask ourselves to explain why we started a business in the first place, "So I could work more hours and enjoy life less" is probably not on that list. I doubt it was on Larry Miller's list. He was a good man and a philanthropist with everything to live for.

Sacrificing your health for your business leads to less physical function, limiting your ability to do the things you love and possibly shortening your life. You're probably thinking, "Wait a minute, Allan, you told me I was going to have to make a lot of sacrifices to start a business. Now, which is it—sacrifice or don't sacrifice?" This is why you have to get those nonnegotiables nailed down early on so you don't overstep your sacrifices and incur permanent damage to what really matters. Don't sacrifice things of greater value for things of lesser value.

My nonnegotiables include my spirituality, my family, and my mental, physical, and emotional health. Your nonnegotiables might be different. But what if one of your other categories—a "non-nonnegitiable," so to speak—supports one of your *nonnegotiables*? For example, you might have a habit of reading for an hour every morning. If that intellectual stimulation helps you function at a higher level, then you might want to hang on to that hobby. But you might have to give up something else of less importance, or spend just half an hour reading, because your time is limited. Similarly, if you pursue hobbies during times when you're most awake and alert, you may have to use that time to run your business and push those hobbies off to other times, when your full attention isn't so critical. Instead of reading for an hour in the morning, you may only be able to read for half an hour at night. Most of us reach a point in the day where we're just not being productive. The law of diminishing returns kicks in, and what would take us an hour to do well now takes two hours to do poorly. Consider moving your hobbies—especially the less physically demanding ones—to those times.

> Don't sacrifice things of greater
> value for things of lesser value.

The benefit of sacrificing hobbies is that you become much more efficient with how you spend your time on recreational activities. You'll realize that some of your hobbies weren't that important to you in the first place, and you may even be relieved to give them up (e.g., going to bars with friends). You will also get back valuable time to spend on your business.

MY JOURNEY TO PROTECTING NONNEGOTIABLES

Once I identified my nonnegotiables, I began trimming away at my hobbies. I couldn't watch a game with my friends every week, live or on TV, anymore. But I was not going to miss my kids' birthdays. I had to be there for them and watch them grow up. When I started my first business, Proof Pest Control, I had a two-year-old and a four-month-old. I wasn't a perfect dad. There were days when I left the house before they got up and came home after they were asleep. Honestly, I'm not proud of that. And there are still days when I get emotional thinking about it. But I was still figuring all this stuff out. It didn't take long for me to get my act together and make a rule for myself that I would never let a day go by when I didn't see my children. Unless I'm on the road for work, I spend time with them in person every day.

A couple of months into that business, after I'd given up sports, I realized how bad I felt physically and emotionally, and so I started going to the gym. I needed something to help me deal with the pressures of starting a business. The effect on my physical and mental well-being was immediate. My stress decreased, I had more energy, and work became less of a burden because I knew I would have that break in the day to turn it off and just work out.

Later, I took up meditation. That was difficult because my mind was always racing, but I learned to clear my thoughts and give myself the mental break my mind craved, preparing myself for all the hard thinking required to run my business.

Now I spend time on myself every day, reading, praying, meditating, and working out. If I miss a day, I don't beat myself up over it, but I make sure not to miss two days in a row. The days when I don't take time to disconnect and recover are harder, so even though I might save some time by skipping those routines, I'm less focused the rest of the day, and everything else takes longer.

A couple of months into my first business, I tried to get my morning routine in place. Since I was busy at home, in the office, and during my commute, I parked my truck at work, and before going inside, I'd go through my meditations and affirmations. It didn't take long for my employees to catch on to my new routine, and eventually they started coming out to my truck to ask me questions. I had to park further away where they wouldn't see me. That was a good temporary solution, but eventually I learned how important these activities were to my recovery. Putting them in my nonnegotiables category wasn't enough—I had to establish boundaries and protect them.

Setting those boundaries is critical because when you start a business, it seems like everything is an emergency. If you are constantly putting out fires, you can't do the real, deep work, and you certainly can't take care of yourself. I didn't figure this out right away, and so getting into a routine and protecting it took more than six months. I had to learn that everything wasn't urgent, some things could wait, and my physical and mental health, my relationships, and even some of my hobbies were higher priorities than my business. In fact, my business would have failed without them.

> Setting those boundaries is critical
> because when you start a business, it
> seems like everything is an emergency.

Once you decide which hobbies, habits, and routines to maintain, clear a path. Make it as easy as possible to stick with them. I began getting up forty-five minutes before the rest of my family, allowing quiet, undisturbed time for meditation, affirmations, and prayer. I spoke with my wife and my children about "office time," when I'm in my home office with the door closed and I cannot be interrupted except for emergencies. Those conversations avoided misunderstandings and hurt feelings, and they also taught my children that it's okay to have "me time."

DON'T WAIT "UNTIL THINGS SLOW DOWN"

Entrepreneurs put off these steps, thinking the demands on their time will diminish over time. They think their schedules will magically self-correct and they'll have time for all those things they sacrificed. Except that time never comes. Not unless you design it and protect it. You will always have more to do than time to do it, so you have to get a handle on this as soon as possible. Otherwise, you'll either sacrifice the wrong things and damage your business and yourself or you won't sacrifice anything, and you'll wonder why your business failed.

Think of this as going from being a bit player in a movie to taking on the starring role or from being a spectator at a football game to being the quarterback. You aren't just running the show—you are the show. As you build your business and hire employees, you'll be able to pass on some responsibilities, but you will always be the last line of defense against every problem and potential failure. This can become a massive burden, and you will need downtime or you'll burn out.

HANG ON TO THE HOBBIES THAT DEFINE YOU

Ideally, the hobbies you hang on to should align with your nonnegotiables. But what about those activities that are near and dear to your heart, those hobbies that define you? For me, that was golf. The thought of giving it up completely really bothered me, but finding a workaround by playing less and playing with one of my kids made it doable.

Other hobbies that I thought were important really weren't. It took some soul-searching to identify those and realize they were wasting my time. Chess was one of those hobbies. I used to play a lot, thinking I enjoyed it and the mental stimulation was good for me. In reality, playing chess was stressful. I took it way too seriously. I was extremely competitive and took a win-at-all-costs approach. What I didn't realize at the time was how many critical decisions are required to play chess well. Sure, you can memorize a lot of moves, but you are still weighing each one in your mind before touching a piece. All that critical thinking and decision-making was draining me, making it harder to make decisions about my business. Worse, the game was affecting me emotionally. I'd get upset when I didn't win, to a point that I won't get into here in detail. Suffice it to say that I was muted for a year because of my overly aggressive "smack talk." Not my proudest moment.

Hobbies are healthy until they become obsessions. Like addictions, they can impact other parts of your life, and so when that happens, you have to let them go.

If games like chess affect you differently, providing a break from work, by all means, keep playing. Just limit your time on them. Set a timer if you have to and commit to playing for just twenty minutes a day, or whatever you can spare.

PROTECT YOUR DISCONNECTING
AND RECOVERY TIME

Research shows that recovery is essential for flow and increased high performance. The value of psychological detachment from work, such as might be gained through hobbies, is one aspect of this principle. The more successful you become, the more critical recovery becomes. As business innovator Dan Sullivan notes, "There's now an entire subsection of occupational psychology growing around the importance of work-recovery called *psychological detachment from work.* True psychological detachment occurs when you completely refrain from work-related activities, as well as obsessive thoughts during non-work time." He further notes that psychological detachment leads to less work-related fatigue and procrastination, increased physical health, greater marital satisfaction, increased overall quality of life, and greater mental health.[10]

Disconnecting from work means just that—doing things that have nothing to do with your business. Playing golf with clients is not disconnecting. You're still "on," still being "the professional," and still thinking about work. Likewise with colleagues—unless you can all agree not to talk about business, going for a hike with your business partners doesn't provide the recovery benefits your mind and body need to perform at their highest levels.

One of my law school buddies, Alex, liked to throw parties, especially around holidays like Halloween. He had a lot of rules, which seemed weird to me at the time, but now I understand why. We weren't allowed to talk about work or school. He enforced the rules with punishments, usually drinking-related, such as having to take a shot. (I can't remember my punishment, considering I don't drink.) I don't recommend this, but you get the idea. Those rules made conversations a little awkward at first—the law was how we had met and how we were all connected. But eliminating the topic made us talk about

---

10   Dan Sullivan and Benjamin Hardy, *10x Is Easier than 2x: How World-Class Entrepreneurs Achieve More by Doing Less* (Hay House, 2023), 184.

other things, so we really got to know each other. The added bonus was that we were able to disconnect and recover mentally from the intensity and strain of work and study.

At the time, I was looking for a job and not having any success. The stress was getting to me, and so not talking about the law for a few hours was a huge relief. I got to know my classmates on a different level, too, and I began interacting with them differently. Without those rules, we instinctively talked about the same topics over and over again, preventing us from really getting to know each other. With those rules in place, every time I began a conversation, I had to think about what I was going to say. The conversations were fresh and more interesting, and it turned out we had more in common than school and the law. Most of the people at these parties were my law school buddies, but there were other people, too, who weren't connected to the law at all. I can't imagine how boring our usual conversations would have been to them! Without those rules, they would have felt very isolated. It would be like going to a party where everyone spoke a different language from yours and you had no idea what they were saying. Full disclosure: the first time I went to one of these parties, I broke the rules at least fifteen times within an hour. It was hard to talk about something other than school! Once I got the hang of it, I was all in.

Even the more difficult sacrifices don't have to be long term. You may only have to give up a hobby for a year or two. Or not give it up completely but just cut back. But the long-term benefits will make that sacrifice worth the expense. The key is being intentional about what you give up, what you keep, and how you manage those hobbies so they don't impact your ability to run your business and, instead, enhance it.

TAKE BACK YOUR TIME

Starting a business is a great time to reevaluate how you spend your time. Let go of those hobbies that don't matter and focus on those that define you, that intersect with your nonnegotiables, and that are critical to your rest and recovery. Remember, you can always pick them back up later when your business is established and you have reached a state of freedom with your time and money.

You will find that some hobbies you thought mattered weren't important at all. That clarity isn't possible when you're in the middle of playing six hours of golf or going at it with an opponent in an online chess game. Trust me, once you let go, you'll wonder why you committed so much time to certain activities in the first place. You'll find that some of your hobbies were simply habits you fell into and there are much better, more productive, and more enjoyable ways to spend time.

Find hobbies that allow you to experience psychological detachment from work. If you like to read, don't read only business books. If you spend time outside the office with your colleagues or your staff, consider spending that time on non-work-related activities, such as playing golf, pool, or even chess, and institute a "no shoptalk" rule.

Cutting out the hobbies that don't serve you gives you more time for your business. Maintaining hobbies that allow you to detach, recharge, and recover will make you more effective with the time you commit to work.

PACK YOUR LUNCH QUESTIONS AND ACTIONS

1. What are you currently trading of greater value for that which has lesser value?
2. What hobbies do you have that serve multiple purposes (mental and physical health, relationships)?
3. Are you disguising any hobbies that are actually work-related/nondetached hobbies?
4. If you could spend some time every day or every week on activities that have nothing at all to do with your work, how might that help your creativity? Your energy? Your attitude toward work? Do you think that solving problems outside of work might prepare you to solve them in your business?

5

YOUR RELATIONSHIPS WILL CHANGE

"The people you start with are not always the ones you end up with, and that's okay."

—ANONYMOUS

One day at church I noticed a young man, a teenager who was part of a family I'd known for a while, head in hands, looking down for the entire hour-long sermon. He didn't raise his eyes even once, and I couldn't tell if he was half asleep or just not interested. He was a good kid, but he had recently stopped enjoying church. His mother made him attend every week (an "under my roof" scenario), but still, I had never seen him so down. I knew he'd recently fallen in with a rough group and wondered if those relationships were contributing to his demeanor.

After the service, I approached him to tell him about my work as a business owner and coach and to see if he needed someone to talk to who wouldn't judge him, but just listen, and maybe offer a bit of advice. He wasn't very open with me, but I could tell something was troubling him. I told him that the next time he was out with his friends, to look around and see who he would most like to become more like. Who among his peers did he see as a role model? Then I suggested if none of his usual friends fit that model, he should look for new friends. He did not take that advice, and within a few months, he was doing hard drugs. His parents kicked him out of the house, and he stopped going to church, so I didn't see him anymore.

Relationships can make or break you, not only as a person but also a business owner. The people with whom you surround yourself can lift you up or drag you down.

Certain events in life serve as natural times for reflection. Sometimes we do this voluntarily, and other times that reflection is necessary. Reflection is mandatory when you start a business. It's critical to review your relationships and decide which ones make sense for the new life you are creating. For the next couple of years, you'll be in a sort of foxhole with these people. Which ones can you continue to support while ensuring your own survival? Who will stick by your side, and who will sabotage you—intentionally or unintentionally? Eventually, you can loosen the constraints and open yourself up to more people, but right now you do not have that luxury. After your nonnegotiables, your business must come first.

A major benefit to culling nonproductive relationships is the time you'll get back to deepen your relationships with the people who matter most. Sharing your business experience, particularly the toughest situations, can strengthen those relationships. According to "Sharing a New Foxhole with Friends: The Impact of Outdoor Recreation on Injured Military," in *Therapeutic Recreation Journal*, studies found that experiencing high-stress situations with someone else can lead to the formation of strong bonds, known as "brotherhood" or "camaraderie," which can help individuals cope with stress and trauma.[11]

---

11   Sharon D. Rogers et al., "Sharing a New Foxhole with Friends: The Impact of Outdoor Recreation on Injured Military," *Therapeutic Recreation Journal* L, no. 3 (2016): 213–227, https://bctra.org/wp-content/uploads/tr_journals/2837-25033-1-PB.pdf.

My wife, for example, has been my best sounding board. She always gives me good advice, and our relationship—tested during those early days—grew stronger with every failure and success, as we realized what was possible if we stuck together, supporting one another's individual dreams. No one starts a business knowing all the answers. Every day, you're solving the next set of problems. Along with the emotional support and encouragement, my wife helped me work through many challenges. I'm not lying when I say that I was genuinely in awe of her at times. Starting a business tested my knowledge and abilities, and it tested hers as well. It brought out sides of us we didn't know existed.

Focusing on the most important relationships also gives you more time for other people who make you a better businessperson—the colleagues, coaches, and mentors who want you to succeed. Because of the demanding, sometimes emotional challenges of starting a business, the people who stick by you during this time could well become lifelong friends.

PEOPLE WILL RESPOND DIFFERENTLY TO YOU, THE BUSINESS OWNER

As you commit time, attention, and resources to your business, your relationships will change. Some people will support you, and others will not. You may have to abandon or limit some relationships while developing new ones. Managing your relationships can determine your growth and your stagnation.

Jim Rohn noted, "You're the average of the five people you spend the most time with."[12] As if by osmosis, we adopt the behaviors and attitudes of these people, perhaps to fit in and also as a survival mechanism, to become part of the tribe and not be left behind.

---

12 Aimee Groth, "You're the Average of the Five People You Spend the Most Time With," *Business Insider* July 2012, https://www.businessinsider.com/jim-rohn-youre-the-average-of-the-five-people-you-spend-the-most-time-with-2012-7.

My family spends our summers in Idaho, where our kids join the local baseball teams. Last summer I was able to help coach my oldest son, Maddox. It was fun, but one of the local teams beat my son's team every time. They were an excellent team—for rural Idaho. But if they were to come to Phoenix to play against more experienced teams, they would be humbled quickly.

Being with people who are less successful, less driven, less educated, and less knowledgeable feels good. That kind of situation makes us feel superior—like a big fish in a small pond. But big fish in small ponds don't grow. To grow and improve, we have to move to bigger ponds and surround ourselves with bigger fish. Sometimes growth requires looking for new people, and if they aren't in your pond, you have to change your environment.

When you start a business, you might be surprised by the responses of the people around you. Don't expect your professional associates, friends, or even your family to get on board with your new venture. Some will merely be unsupportive, while others, surprisingly enough, will actively root against you. This came as a complete shock the first time I realized it. They'll discourage you. Not because they suddenly don't like you. They fear how your changes will affect the relationship they have with you, which they value. They also want to protect you, and they are worried about what will happen if you fail. Your risk becomes their risk, in a way, and they are not ready to take on all that uncertainty. Even when you are successful, expect some backlash.

Katherine Newman's ethnographic study *No Shame in My Game: The Working Poor in the Inner City* showed that successful individuals who come from low-income backgrounds may face negative reactions from their families, including feelings of betrayal or jealousy. These dynamics can lead to conflicts and a lack of support from family members.[13]

This may come as a surprise, but negative responses are prevalent among family members. I'm not talking about your spouse—you

---

13   Katherine S. Newman, *No Shame in My Game: The Working Poor in the Inner City* (Knopf Doubleday, 2000).

should have deep discussions about this choice with the people with whom you share a household and who depend on your financial and emotional support. I'm talking about your parents, siblings, aunts, uncles, and anyone close enough to feel as if they are part of your family. These are the people most likely to tell you not to do it. They'll give you every reason in the world why quitting your job and/or starting a business is a horrible idea. But they aren't necessarily turning on you. They care about you and are expressing concern for what they see as a major shift in your profession and who you will ultimately become, which affects them.

> Don't expect your professional associates,
> friends, or even your family to get on board
> with your new venture. Some will merely
> be unsupportive, while others, surprisingly
> enough, will actively root against you.

However, some people have more selfish reasons for dissuading your entrepreneurial ambitions. They don't want you to succeed, fearing your success will make them appear less successful. My rule of thumb when someone gives me advice about starting another business is to consider where they are in their professional life. Has their approach worked for them? Would I trade places with them professionally? The answer is usually no, but sometimes it's yes. It's sort of like when you're at the gym and someone who's terribly out of shape tries to give you workout advice. How can you trust what they say?

You will have to decide which relationships to keep and which to limit or abandon. People to keep in your circle are those who believe in you and maybe want to be like you. You might become a role model to them. You could end up mentoring them down the road, or even hiring them to work for your business. I coach and mentor employees and clients all the time. It's part of my job as a business owner and a professional business consultant. I learn from them because I'm naturally curious and they have a different perspective from mine, but I am mostly there to instruct.

You'll also have to seek out new people who might serve as mentors and role models—fish that are bigger than you, in ponds bigger than yours. My mentors and the people I surround myself with are generally at or above my professional level. I choose those relationships carefully. Again, time is a limited resource, more so for new business owners.

PRIORITIZING RELATIONSHIPS

Analyzing and prioritizing your relationships may seem cold and impersonal, but if you don't take a hard look at the people you spend time with, you'll give too much of yourself to people who hold you back. Here's how I categorize my relationships:

#1: FIRST ARE THE NONNEGOTIABLE RELATIONSHIPS.

For me, this includes my immediate family—my wife and children. I protect those relationships and don't sacrifice them for any others. Your nonnegotiable relationships may be with different people, but the prioritization and protection is the same.

The effort you put into finding a spouse or best friend and gaining one another's trust doesn't guarantee they'll hang around forever. It's not like buying a car, where you pay it off and it's yours. You have to continually invest in that relationship. If you're a parent, your relationships with your children are even more critical because they grow and change so quickly. A week away from your spouse is one thing—a week away from you one-year-old and you could miss their first words, first tooth, first steps. You can't make up for lost time with nonnegotiable relationships.

Here's a secret: you're in a much better position to start and operate a business when things are right at home. A happy home allows you to focus on work when you're there instead of worrying about what's going on with your spouse and kids.

Single and childless people have nonnegotiable relationships with parents, siblings, and best friends. These are the people you can be vulnerable with and who will not judge you. You might even include a pet as a nonnegotiable. Your dog may not help you with problem-solving, but they rely on you for food and shelter, and you rely on them for companionship and emotional support.

> You're in a much better position to start and operate a business when things are right at home.

#2: ONCE YOU'VE IDENTIFIED YOUR CORE NONNEGOTIABLE RELATIONSHIPS, CONSIDER THE OTHER PEOPLE IN YOUR LIFE.

Which relationships should you limit, and which should you end? You have to make some hard decisions about how much time you'll spend with other people, who could be the people you spend the most time with now. Some of those relationships may not be in the best interest of your business or you, as a business owner. This step is difficult. We all have people in our lives who don't contribute to our happiness or success. Some of these people are sort of "neutral"; they don't necessarily work against us, but they don't have much to offer either. Still others are disruptive or even toxic.

The low-hanging fruit are the negative people that drain you emotionally and mentally. These people are everywhere—on social media, in professional networking groups, in homeowners' associations...but you don't have to associate with them. Just because you joined a group doesn't mean you have to participate, especially if it means exposing yourself to narcissists, manipulators, and constant complainers. People who are always asking you for something and never giving anything back can suck up a lot of time. Those are the relationships you must limit or eliminate completely, depending on the individual and your relationship to them. Stop responding to their text messages, or wait a few days to respond. Limit your participation in groups that don't help you, or quit them.

This process isn't easy and can be complicated when your non-negotiable people, such as brothers and sisters, don't support your business and the people you need to limit your time with do. You still need people in your life who believe in what you're doing. You can't just divorce your in-laws. Your banker/accountant/lawyer may be irritating at times, but you need them. While you're evaluating relationships, you might discover people you overlooked who should be added to your core nonnegotiable group. Maybe your gym buddies or the guys in your running group. Or other entrepreneurs you met in an online forum or a mastermind. Even the guys you play basketball with one night a week. These people aren't critical to your business success, but they may be necessary to your physical and mental health.

#3: WHEN YOU UNDERTAKE A MAJOR CHANGE LIKE STARTING A BUSINESS, PEOPLE WILL GIVE YOU ADVICE THAT PROTECTS THEM, NOT YOU.

They don't want their lives to change. They do not want to lose you, a member of their "tribe." Think about that as you consider your relationships. They may not come right out and say, "Are you sure you want to start a business?" Instead, they'll say, "Are you sure you want to quit being a _____?" Don't be surprised if it's your mom or dad saying this to you. They may think they're acting in your best interest, but they don't know what's in your heart and your head, and they cannot make this decision for you. Expect to hear this, and prepare yourself so you don't take these comments personally. Understand where they're coming from. Be ready for it. Say something like "Hey, I love you and respect your opinion. But I am going to do what I believe is best for me and my family, and I need you to support me in this decision."

By the way, these people's attitudes toward your decision may never change. So limit how much you share with them about your business. Some of the most important communication skills we learn involve what *not* to tell certain people. They are telling you how they feel about it—believe them. If you then vent to them every time you have a problem with your business, they will remind you that they knew it was a bad idea right from the start. If you need to vent, vent to the right people. Some people will try to solve your problem, which you may not want—you may just need to vent. Others will say "I told you so." Still others will listen, understanding what you need, listening and not judging. You need someone like that in your life. Just be sure to reciprocate when they come to you with their problems.

I want to share one of the most difficult issues that I have faced. My in-laws boycotted my wedding. A few of my wife's relatives showed up, but some of them—including her father—bowed out. I couldn't understand why they wouldn't attend one of the most important days in their daughter's life. Years later, my wife and I finally connected the pieces. Before we were married and early in our relationship, my wife confided details about me to her sister. She wasn't sure about me— didn't know if I was mature enough for a real relationship or whether I'd be truly committed to a marriage. She didn't think I was "marriage material." Honestly, I probably wasn't at the time, but I grew up fast, and marrying her was the best decision I ever made. But back then, her sister and the rest of her family questioned my motives and my dedication. They didn't believe I could be trusted with the future happiness of one of the most important people in their lives. Unfortunately, that belief persisted. They had heard so many of my wife's misgivings that they weren't ready to turn on a dime and accept me into the fold.

My in-laws saw me as a threat to their family, and it took them a while to come around. That experience taught me an important lesson that I've counted on in my business relationships. I'm careful about sharing negative news. Human beings are very sensitive to anything that threatens them. Think about it—when you watch or read the news, do you tune in to the good news, or is the bad news more likely to grab your attention? There's a reason there are no "good news reports" every evening. The ratings would nose-dive, and the stations would lose all their advertising. The networks may air a short, positive story at the end of the broadcast, but for the most part, they only give us the threats because that's what we want to know. (Seriously, do you want to know about the sunshine coming in from the east or the tornado coming from the west? About the car accident blocking the freeway on your route to work or the fact that a million other people traveled the same highway this morning without incident?)

There is nothing wrong with venting—as long as you don't let it go on too long—and if you keep your problems in perspective and balance them with the positives. You can't let one bad customer experience ruin your whole day, and if it helps to talk about it to someone, don't walk out onto the office floor and complain to anyone who'll listen. You might save that conversation for your spouse or a business partner but include the upside too. "Yeah, I had this one bad experience, but here's what I learned from it, and here's a good experience I had today." Otherwise, whomever you complain to will have the impression that your business is one big disaster. They'll think *you* are one big disaster, and they will not show up for your wedding.

#4: REDUCING OR ELIMINATING YOUR TIME
WITH SOME PEOPLE GIVES YOU MORE TIME
TO DEEPEN IMPORTANT RELATIONSHIPS AND
DEVELOP NEW ONES WITH PEOPLE WHO ARE
INTERESTED IN YOU AND YOUR BUSINESS.

Instead of holding you back, these people help you move forward.

Again, I know this sounds harsh. But think about the last time you moved. Do you remember sorting through your stuff and thinking, "Why am I hanging on to this? Do I really want to pack it up and move it to another place?" You probably threw a lot of it away or donated it to Goodwill. I'm not comparing people to electronics that don't work and clothes that don't fit, but if a relationship is taking up space in your life, toss it out and recapture that space so you can fill it up with something better. You might be amazed by how much time you spend with people who slow your progress and prevent you from succeeding. That time could be spent with a business coach, a mentor, or a mastermind. Like Chase Jarvis, photographer and founder of CreativeLive, says in *Never Play It Safe*, "Though everyone is deserving of kindness, not everyone is deserving of your focus or friendship."[14]

#5: YOU WILL SACRIFICE TIME WITH MANY RELATIONSHIPS SO YOU DON'T HAVE TO SACRIFICE (MUCH) TIME WITH THE FEW MOST IMPORTANT RELATIONSHIPS.

When you are with the people who really matter, make the most of that time by being present. When you spend time with people, especially those people in your core group, make that time count. Make eye contact. Listen. Be present. We've all heard about the importance of mindfulness and being in the moment (instead of using that time to regret the past and worry about the future). This concept is even more important when you are sharing time with another person. That time is precious, but only if you make it so.

You cannot skim over relationships and expect to make up that lost time later. So don't think you can work really hard for three years to ensure future financial freedom for yourself and your family, sacrificing time with them in the process. You will never have that opportunity. Sure, you can keep up with old friends and colleagues with periodic outreach, but the core relationships must be tended to

---

14   Chase Jarvis, *Never Play It Safe: A Practical Guide to Freedom, Creativity, and a Life You Love* (Harper, 2024), 52.

consistently. This topic is near and dear to me because, though I feel as if I did my best with what I knew at the time, I wish I had fully grasped the importance of spending time with my kids earlier in my career. It's one of the regrets I have as a business owner, and I hate seeing other entrepreneurs make this mistake. If you feel like you've fallen into this trap, it's not too late to do something about it. Commit to change right now, today. Put your core relationships on your calendar if that helps. Schedule a weekly date night with your spouse, morning and nightly routines with your kids, and regular family outings. Sharing time with them consistently won't only improve those relationships; it will also make you a happier person who's better equipped to focus on work when you are at work.

How you spend that time depends on the person. One of my sons likes to play sports like golf, while my other son prefers video games. So when I spend time with them individually, I put my preferences aside and consider their perspectives. This takes some emotional intelligence, which does not always come naturally, but you can develop it. Before you schedule dinner at a Thai restaurant (knowing your spouse loves Italian food) or you buy tickets to a football game (when your daughter's an avid soccer fan), put yourself in their shoes and consider how they would like to spend your time together.

LONG-TERM FOCUSED BALANCE

In *Procrastinate on Purpose*, Rory Vaden introduces the idea of embracing the "focused imbalance."[15] I don't believe anyone can live a truly balanced life in the literal sense of the term—balance implies assigning equal weight to items on a scale. In the short term, you will have to spend more time launching and running your business than you did in a regular job. Likewise, when you're on vacation, you're (hopefully) not devoting equal time to your business. You're trying to leave the office behind to focus on family, friends, and recreation in a new location.

---

15 Rory Vaden, *Procrastinate on Purpose: 5 Permissions to Multiply Your Time* (Penguin, 2015).

Think about balance more in a long-term sense, where some days call for more time and work, while other days call for more personal time. Think about balance over the course of ten or twenty years, not over this week. If you don't think about it this way, you'll be racked with guilt, especially on those days when you had to put in twelve long hours and you weren't able to tend to personal responsibilities and relationships. Give yourself some grace. Your kids will understand if you miss dinner with them one night—just don't miss dinner two nights in a row, and certainly don't make it a habit.

> Think about balance over the course of ten or twenty years, not over this week.

Before you launch your business, establish rules that work for you and your core relationships. Within your nonnegotiable relationships, set rules for your interactions with the people and things you care about most. For example, commit to being home for dinner with the family for a minimum of five nights a week. Commit to attending church every Sunday, no matter what's going on at your business. Commit to never missing your kids' birthdays or your anniversary. Agree to a "no cell phones at the dinner table" rule. Have conversations about how your life is going to change and how that will affect the people you care about most. Set those expectations, and ask for their support. And when you have an extra-busy day or week coming up, talk to those people about it so they know it's coming and won't be caught off guard. People tend not to like surprises, especially negative surprises that impact their plans, but if you give them time to prepare, they're a lot more understanding.

You are one human being, and you are asking a lot of yourself. But with the support of your core group, you can accomplish your goals while keeping important relationships intact and even improving them.

When I talk about nonnegotiables, I'm usually referring to my wife, my children, and a few relatives, colleagues, and close friends. They all provide me with something I need (and vice versa), and so when I'm establishing new relationships, I tend to gravitate toward people who offer something else. Our relationship needs may be different, so be aware of what's missing in your life and who might fill that need. Maybe you're looking to expand your professional network. Or you have too many people in your life, and you prefer to spend more time with a select group. You could be seeking a mentor or a mentee—someone to train who can fill in for you when you need a week off. Before looking for new people, take another look at the people around you. They may have the ability to fill those roles, but you haven't given them the chance. Other people may be satisfied in the roles they've taken on in your life. They're happy to be your employees, but they don't want to come to your house for a barbecue on Saturday. Again, this comes down to emotional intelligence and seeing the world from points of view beyond your own. Sharpen that skill, and the relationships you need will flourish.

PACK YOUR LUNCH—AND YOUR PEOPLE

Your relationships will change, and this will happen quickly. Get ahead of this change by identifying the relationships that should not be sacrificed, then commit to them and to nonnegotiables within them. Protect them. Identify people to keep in your life but who may get less time, and figure out who is holding you back, not providing any benefit, and should be cut from your life completely. Then think about new relationships you should cultivate.

Remember that this is not a permanent situation. Reevaluate your relationships during these initial years as a business owner and decide if your choices are working for you. If they are not, make changes. After your first year as business owner, you may have more time and can start socializing more with people outside your core group. You may discover a weakness in your knowledge and skills and decide to join a group or hire a coach that can help fill that gap.

The people you spend time with can have the greatest impact on your physical and mental health. They will affect your success. Choose carefully; avoid regrets. If you choose these sacrifices intentionally, your relationships with the people who matter most to you will grow stronger. Those people will witness your hard work and your commitment to them, and they will support you and provide stability on this journey. You need people like this in your life, especially when you take on the demands of starting a business.

PACK YOUR LUNCH QUESTIONS AND ACTIONS

1. Who are the nonnegotiable people in your life?
2. What daily and weekly events can you commit to *never* missing?
3. Do you have relationships that need to be limited or even removed from your life?

6

YOU WILL HAVE TO SACRIFICE THE PLEASURE OF DISTRACTION

"In the absence of disciplined focus, we become strangely loyal to performing daily acts of trivia."

—ROBERT A. HEINLEIN

An individual came to me for advice. He plopped a huge green notebook on my desk, turned it facing toward me, and flipped through the pages.

"What's all this?" I asked.

"Well," he said, "I have a lot of business ideas, and I don't know which ones to pursue."

The guy had over fifty business concepts. I wasn't going to read his entire notebook, but I asked him to describe a few of his favorites—the ones he was most excited about and that he thought had the most potential.

Some of them were good, some bad, some so-so. But none of that mattered. What mattered was that he pick one and go for it.

I told him, "Okay, how about picking the one you really want to do right now? Then take this notebook and put it up on a really high shelf. For the next three to four years, focus all of your efforts on that one idea. Pretend those other ones don't exist. Then, when that one business succeeds and is able to run and grow without you, take the notebook down and pick another idea."

He said he'd give it a shot. I watched his progress through the years, and it was clear that he couldn't build a single business. If you can't build one business at a time, you can't build fifty businesses. It's as simple as that. Start with one. Learn. Improve. Get really good at it, so good you don't have to be in the business every day running it. Watch it grow without you. Then think about starting another one.

> If you can't build one business at a time, you can't build fifty businesses.

Any business, and especially a new business, takes time. You have to put your heart and soul into it. It's tough to get a business off the ground, and anything that takes you away from it decreases the chances of success. You can do that with one business, but not two, and certainly not more than two. It's like launching a rocket—you're fighting the forces of gravity, and that takes every bit of thrust you can muster to get it off the ground.

Starting a second business diverts that thrust, and your first rocket plunges back to Earth. Your second rocket may never leave the ground. It's the same with side hustles—those businesses you think you can launch in your spare time, after business hours. You need that time for your nonnegotiables. You need it to recover from the intensity of your new business. But you need it for something else too: in that downtime, you're problem-solving, thinking about how to fix issues and improve your business. Yes, psychological detachment from your business is critical to your mental health. But sometimes allowing yourself some mental space during "downtime" to sort out a problem can be very effective. Let your mind wander, talk to your friends and family members about what you're doing, and a solution will come to you. You don't always have the luxury of time for that kind of thinking and those conversations when you're working in the business. How you spend your time both on the clock and off the clock contributes to the thrust you need to get the business off the ground and propel it to success. Keep in mind that you still need to practice psychological detachment from work, as discussed in Chapter 4.

Entrepreneurs underestimate how much time it takes to get off the ground. They think they can just set up a business and everything will run like clockwork. That's not how it works. Things will go wrong, and you need time to make mistakes, learn from them, iterate, and try something else. You need deliberate dedication to one business, continually trying one thing after another to see what works. There is no step-by-step or color-by-number process for business success. Every business, every business owner, and every market is different, and that means different problems and solutions. No matter how prepared you think you are, you're still learning a lot through trial and error, and for those initial years, you can only keep your eye on one company at a time. There are many moving pieces and a lot of unpredictability, and you don't know what you don't know until you're in the middle of it.

YOU DON'T KNOW WHAT YOU DON'T KNOW

My son started playing tackle football this year, and I volunteered to help coach. To prepare, I watched football health and safety videos. Since I haven't played football in a long time, I figured a lot had changed, and I wanted to be up to date on things like concussion protocol.

Even though I played for eight years, including all through high school, I figured I'd brush up on the fundamentals and logistics, so I watched training videos on those subjects. They covered techniques for blocking, tackling, and other maneuvers that I did for years and apparently—I realized after watching these videos—knew nothing about! Maybe there are better resources for kids nowadays, but the point is that I played for years and have been watching the game for decades, and I'm amazed by how much I don't know.

In *Outliers: The Story of Success*, Malcolm Gladwell's "10,000-Hour Rule" suggests that mastering a skill requires ten thousand hours of practice, yet the success of the Beatles, as discussed by Gladwell, was not solely achieved through practice; it also necessitated the influence of family, culture, and personal development beyond the workplace, highlighting that success is a multifaceted journey.[16]

"Making smaller circles," a concept by Josh Waitzkin, emphasizes that mastery is achieved by deconstructing complex skills into their most basic elements, perfecting these fundamentals through intensive practice, and then integrating them into more advanced techniques, leading to a deep, intuitive understanding and enhanced overall performance.[17] How many entrepreneurs take that kind of time to launch a business? More often, we jump into the deep end and figure it out along the way.

When I lived in Michigan, I went to a University of Michigan football game at the stadium there, commonly known as "the Big House." As luck would have it, I sat next to a former starting quarterback of the opposing team. He had played recently and knew all the play calls, and as he talked with his buddy, I realized he was watching the signs from the play coach to the quarterback and predicting every play before they snapped the ball. He said things like "That guy screwed up—he was supposed to be five yards out, not eight." This former player saw so much that I had missed because I didn't know what to look for.

---

16   Malcolm Gladwell, *Outliers: The Story of Success* (Little, Brown, 2008).

17   Josh Waitzkin, *The Art of Learning: An Inner Journey to Optimal Performance* (Free Press, 2007).

Because he had played, he knew what was going to happen next and what could go wrong. You need that same kind of intelligence, and you can't build it trying to focus on two businesses at once. You must make smaller circles.

In his book *Deep Work*, Cal Newport suggests that there are two core abilities for thriving: "1. The ability to quickly master hard things. 2. The ability to produce at an elite level, in terms of both quality and speed." A prerequisite to both of these is the ability to avoid distractions.[18]

People know a lot about their current occupations. They understand the training and experience it took to get good at what they do. For some reason, entrepreneurs don't understand being a business owner is a whole new occupation that demands just as much training and experience as being whoever they were in their previous career. The difference is that most entrepreneurs learn as they go instead of studying business for six years, doing an internship, and then launching their first company.

Running a business requires a lot of busywork—tasks that don't take a lot of thinking but need to be done. It also requires deep work. Deep work can only be accomplished with intense focus and no distractions. Entering a state of mind where you are capable of deep work isn't instantaneous. It takes a while to get to that state of being 100 percent honed in and fully focused. If you're distracted, you can't get right back into that state either. You need time to get back into it.

TAKING OWNERSHIP OF YOUR ATTENTION

As a new business owner—even after you've hired people to help you—you are still involved in everything. You answer the phones and emails; monitor the company's social media, marketing, advertising, and reviews; do payroll; pay vendors; hire, train, and manage more people. You turn on the lights in the morning and turn them off at

---

18   Cal Newport, *Deep Work: Rules for Focused Success in a Distracted World* (Hachette, 2016), 29.

night. Sometimes you take out the trash. Everyone wants to talk to you because you are the person in charge. You can rein in the chaos with scheduling, calendaring, setting boundaries around times you're available, setting rules for acceptable methods of communication (e.g., who can call and text you), and plain old saying no. For now, understand that until you have mastered those skills, you'll be juggling way more than you can handle. There is no room for distractions. The quarterback at that Michigan game saw things I couldn't because he had spent a significant amount of time in deep, focused, uninterrupted work. You also need that time to see things you won't see if you're constantly distracted.

The quote "The greatest asset of the 21st century is the ability to control your attention" is often attributed to Yuval Noah Harari, a historian and author known for his works such as *Sapiens: A Brief History of Humankind* and *21 Lessons for the 21st Century*. Harari has frequently discussed how attention is a crucial resource in the modern age, where technology and media are constantly vying for our focus.[19]

You will have to sacrifice the pleasure of distraction to make room for what's important to your business. You need that time and focus to improve as a business owner and to improve and grow your business. So while it may be tempting to answer emails and scroll through your business's reviews and comments on your social media accounts, dedicating more time to the bigger problems and less time to the smaller ones yields better results. Like not going out of business.

Consider the research that goes into developing social media, marketing, and advertising, which are all designed to grab and hold your attention, essentially stealing time away from what you should be doing. Breaking the phone-checking habit is especially difficult. According to an article published by Piedmont Healthcare, when we check our phones, our brains release a small amount of dopamine. Dopamine motivates us to take action, and each time we hear a notification, we check our device. The problem is this dopamine boost is

---

19   Yuval Noah Harari, *21 Lessons for the 21st Century* (Spiegel & Grau, 2018).

temporary and leads to a letdown. Our brains want more dopamine, which triggers the habit of checking our phones constantly throughout the day.[20]

We've all heard the philosophy of paying yourself first that's popular in finance. The idea is to put money away for yourself before you pay anyone else. The reason why this is important is because others (creditors) will remind you to pay them. But who is reminding you to pay yourself?

The same concept is true of doing hard work without distractions. Easy work comes with constant reminders—the phone ringing, the text messages pinging—but the hard work typically does not. No one will make you do it, but your business will fail if you don't.

In his landmark book *The 7 Habits of Highly Effective People*, Stephen Covey lays out the four ways we spend time in the time management matrix. The four quadrants include (1) important/urgent; (2) important/not urgent; (3) not important/urgent; and (4) not important/not urgent. Surprisingly, he recommends business leaders spend the majority of their time in the important/not urgent quadrant.[21] This is the work that will make the greatest difference to your business, yet it's the work we all avoid. No one is standing over us telling us to get it done. We must make the mental shift from "employee" to "boss" and insist that this work be done.

SHOW UP AND GO DEEP

If we learn to avoid those attention-stealers and focus on the work that gets us closer to achieving our goals, we will have mastered a skill that sets us head and shoulders above the competition.

When I started practicing law, one of the partners, who was also one of my bosses, said, "You'd be surprised by how much credit you

---

20 "Seven Reasons to Break Your Smartphone Addiction," Piedmont Healthcare, accessed November 27, 2024, https://www.piedmont.org/living-real-change/does-your-smartphone-cause-anxiety.

21 Stephen R. Covey, *The 7 Habits of Highly Effective People: Powerful Lessons in Personal Change* (Simon & Schuster, 1989).

get and how far you get in this business just by showing up." I thought he was being funny, but over time, I realized he was right. Many people, by allowing their focus to be siphoned off, don't really show up. Not 100 percent. They may be there physically, but their minds are someplace else. According to a 2019 survey, 90 percent of all text messages are read within three minutes of being received.[22] How can anyone focus while monitoring text messages?

The deep versus wide concept shows up everywhere—it's how we find and target customers with niche products that satisfy niche needs for niche customers. It's how we write books like this one. There's a saying that if you write a book for everyone, you are really writing a book for no one, and it's the same with your business. The irony is that by going deep, you will be so good at something that you will attract a wider audience than you would have if you had targeted that audience in the first place.

The value of going deep versus going wide cannot be overstated. This applies to staying focused and getting very good at your business, and it also applies to focusing on one business at a time. That means avoiding shiny object syndrome, what I call "the entrepreneur's conundrum," that plagues so many entrepreneurs.

DISTRACTIONS OUTSIDE OF THE BUSINESS: THE ENTREPRENEUR'S CONUNDRUM

Entrepreneurs want to chase every opportunity. We all have a bad case of shiny object syndrome. If this sounds like you, congratulations: you're an entrepreneur.

Launching a business takes all your attention. In those first years, so much can go wrong, and without diligence and all your attention, it will be hard to fix everything. You can avoid many problems by giving your business the attention it requires, which means (outside of your nonnegotiables) almost all of it.

---

22   Piedmont, "Seven Reasons."

Launching a business and getting it to the point where it can grow without you, the founder, takes years. It's not as simple as forming an LLC and setting up a website. I guarantee it's going to be more work than you expect, demanding more time than you plan to give. You have to sacrifice distractions—especially the urge to start another business while the first one is in its infancy.

We have only so much mental capacity, and we know that true multitasking isn't possible. When you do two things at once, you're simply switching between thoughts and activities, and that mental switch takes time. You may not realize it because that time is so minuscule, but it exists, and over hours of work, it adds up. Add to that the time to refocus and you can see how a lot of time is wasted "multitasking." Another thing that happens is that you can't switch between tasks and achieve the mental state required for deep work, so the work you do is inferior. Of course, we can participate in more than one mindless task at a time—eating popcorn while watching television, for example. I'm talking about doing real work, like running two businesses. The standard is "Does it require focus?" If two tasks require focus, they cannot be done at the same time.

It's no surprise that shiny object syndrome is common among entrepreneurs. We're visionaries, constantly asking, "What if?" We're suckers for good ideas, and when we get one, we can't let go. Exploring the possibilities lights up our brains.

DISTRACTIONS WITHIN THE BUSINESS: HOW WE AVOID THE HARD WORK

We are also drawn to distractions within our business. Running a business is hard, and there is so much to do that we are drawn to whatever is easiest and gives us the most immediate sense of accomplishment. This allows us to avoid the hard stuff while justifying our actions and telling ourselves we were still getting something done that had to be done.

DISTRACTIONS ARE MORE PREVALENT
AND HARDER TO AVOID

Technology has created a proliferation of distractions in recent years. We didn't always carry cell phones that allowed people to call, text, email, and message us 24/7. We didn't always feel as if we were expected to respond to phone calls and social media messages right away. We adopted the tech that distracts us without realizing its impact and before we had a chance to develop behaviors to manage it.

We can control those distractions manually or use technology such as Screen Time and other features to help manage them. All the apps on my phone, other than the actual phone function and my calendar, are automatically disabled from 10:00 p.m. until 7:00 a.m. so I'm not tempted to check email or social accounts. I have time limits set on some of my apps, too, so I don't end up going down rabbit holes when I should be working or spending time with the people who matter most.

Marketers thrive on their access to us. Not so long ago, they had only TV, radio, newspaper, magazine, billboard, and phone book (remember those?) ads to attract people, but now they can grab your attention anywhere just by pinging your phone. Marketers and the social media platforms they use compete for your attention. They fill your pages with ads under the guise of "showing you what you want to see," as if you didn't know how to find this stuff yourself. They steal precious minutes that quickly become hours of your time—time your business needs from you to survive. At the same time, anyone with your cell number or email address or who's in your social media circles can interact with you at any time unless you block them. Compare this to the pre-internet years when you interacted with, at most, a couple of hundred people a year. Before cell phones, people had no problem at all ignoring a phone call or letting calls go to voicemail. We've been trained to respond to everything all the time, and we have to discipline ourselves to break that habit.

Constant distractions can also cause a decrease in your attention span, and you need to retain and build on your ability to focus to do the intense critical thinking work required to launch a business. Imagine running your business and playing Whac-A-Mole at the same time. That's what it's like when you give in to distractions. You need that brainpower because you're going to run into problems you've never dealt with before, and you will not have all the answers at first. No matter how many books you read, including this one, you will run into situations you didn't expect.

TECHNIQUES FOR MANAGING DISTRACTIONS

Every time your cell phone pings, or you get a text or an email, or you take a minute away from the task at hand to scroll through Instagram, you are interrupting the flow of thought and taking yourself out of the mental state that took a while to get into. Then, when you go back to it, you have to start all over again. You don't always realize the delay, but it takes time to get back to where you were. Business owners don't have that time to waste, so we have to be extremely efficient.

When you're trying to do something hard, scrolling through social media is tempting. So is answering email. Those are easy tasks that don't require a lot of brainpower. Deep work is hard. It burns calories, and your body fights to conserve calories. Why burn calories on all that hard stuff when it can relax, conserve calories, and do something mindless? You have to control yourself, though, and focus on the task at hand.

When I'm working out at the gym and someone stops to chat, I happily slow down and talk with them. Do you know why? Because it's easier than working out. I justify it by saying I'm being a nice person, and besides, I like talking to that person, but you can't justify those kinds of interruptions at work.

Likewise, when I'm struggling with a tough problem at work and I get a task related to an easier problem, I breathe a huge sigh of relief. "Oh good, I don't have to solve the big problem right now. I can take care of this tiny little problem (which I should probably pass off to someone else) and feel justified in my decision to avoid the big one."

No. Wrong answer. I know this when I do it, and so I have to fight that urge. The best way is by limiting how and when people can contact me. It's like cutting down on sweets—don't buy them and they won't end up in your refrigerator or kitchen cabinets. Miraculous, isn't it?

Another technique to manage distractions is setting aside time for deep work and protecting that time from interruptions. Block out half a day to solve your biggest problems. Remove all distractions during that time—no social media, no internet (other than whatever you need to research the problem and solutions), no email, and no phone calls. If you have an assistant, let them know you are not to be disturbed unless it's an emergency. If you work in an office, close the door and put a sign out front that you are doing deep work and are not to be disturbed. By the way, if you have employees who must do deep work, support them. Guide them on how to achieve that kind of work, show them how to protect their deep work time, and respect their boundaries too.

BUILDING PROCESSES AND SYSTEMS TAKES DISTRACTION-FREE BRAINPOWER

You'll also run into situations you should expect because they come up again and again. Creating good processes and systems to manage recurring events will make your business more efficient. Following those processes and systems takes less brainpower, but developing them requires a lot of thought. Otherwise, you'll have bad systems. Say you run out of butter every week, and so every week you call your butter guy. His number's on a sticky note on your laptop. That's a bad system. The note could get lost. You could run out of butter while someone else who doesn't have your laptop, is minding the store. That's why you need good, foolproof systems developed deliberately to save time and make your business run efficiently.

The butter supply is a simple problem, and you'll come up with a simple system. You'll have more complex problems, such as managing financial statements. I identify financial problems with macrodata, and I have a system for that, which I developed during uninterrupted distraction-free time. Otherwise, I'd be buried in numbers and struggle to find the meaning. Not an efficient way to run a business. I solve those problems with microdata, and again, I need uninterrupted time to do that.

When you go to work for someone else, they have systems in place. You learn them and follow them. When you start a business, you have to create those systems from scratch. You can't do that kind of work while your phone's buzzing.

MICRO AND MACRO DISTRACTIONS

The phone ringing is a micro distraction, but those tiny disruptions pile up, tempting you away from the important work. Micro distractions are tempting because they pull you away from work that takes a lot of thought and toward something that takes little thought. Reading a text while you're trying to write a sales script, for example.

But even macro distractions like starting a second business can be attractive to the entrepreneur. Once you've put a few months into starting the first one, you feel as if you know enough to start another one and so you can just reimplement all that you've learned over the past months. But that takes you away from the first business, so you essentially stop learning how to keep building and improving it, and you never get to a point where it grows without you.

We're infatuated with new ideas, and that honeymoon phase is so fun. Why not repeat it and leave the hard work for...later? We're also prone to a "grass is greener" attitude, thinking this other business will be easier than the first one. False. The other one will be just as hard, and putting off the hard work of the first one will make it impossible to have one, never mind two, good businesses.

PRIORITY DILUTION

I have a detailed calendar of everything I intend to do each day. I block out time to record podcasts, meet with colleagues and staff, review financials, read company email, and other business activities, and I also include things like going to the gym. If I actually stick to my calendar, I accomplish an amazing amount of work. Throughout the day, people and technology vie for my attention.

According to Rory Vaden in his book *Take the Stairs*, "Priority dilution is most commonly found in high-performing people—the ones who are the most busy, competent, and overwhelmed. They know what their goals are—but they nonetheless allow their attention to shift to less important tasks."[23]

Surprisingly, priority dilution is common among high performers. People who are competent and always busy, but who seem to get overwhelmed. They have goals, and they chase them, but they also allow distractions to get in the way. Then, because they're so goal-oriented and driven, they still manage to do the important work. They just don't do a very good job, at least they don't do it as well as they could if they had eliminated the distractions.

Email is the first offender. I've been guilty of using email as a to-do list, waiting for messages to respond to, as if I didn't have a million other things to do. Email is easy. It's that other stuff that's hard, but that other stuff has to be done, or I won't have a business. I'm not saying that email is bad. It's necessary. When you write an email, you have a reason to write it: you need something from someone, or you need to give someone information. But when you're sitting at your desk waiting for email, you're putting your priorities aside to focus on someone else's. Social media is even worse. If you're sitting on your Facebook, Instagram, X, or Threads account waiting for people to like your post, what the heck are you doing? The deep work, that important/not urgent work that you should spend the majority of your time on is bumped for not important (and probably not urgent)

---

23   Rory Vaden, *Take the Stairs: 7 Steps to Achieving True Success* (TarcherPerigree, 2012), 80.

activities. The quote "The most important skill for the next generation of knowledge workers is not learning what to do, but rather learning what not to do," which is often attributed to Peter Drucker (though the source is unclear), is relevant here.

I was on a podcast where the host asked me about work/life balance. As mentioned above, I don't think there is such a thing, because balance implies assigning equal importance to whatever you're weighing. I do believe in being as present as possible with the people you care about.

This is tough for new business owners. We're so worried that something will go wrong. When I started out, I would freak out over every bad review. One day when I was sitting in church, I glanced at my phone and noticed a one-star review. I immediately stepped outside to call the customer. Obviously, that behavior doesn't align with my seven life categories and their priorities. Honestly, did I think the customer was sitting around waiting for a response? Doubtful. Could it have waited until the next day, Monday? Likely. But that's not how new entrepreneurs think. We're the last line of defense between having a successful business and being complete failures, so we tend to be not just responsive but reactive.

It bears repeating: multitasking doesn't work. You can't listen to a sermon and call customers at the same time. You also cannot spend quality time with your family and look at your phone. More than once, I've tried to respond to emails and hold conversations with my children. They know, and they are offended. Don't do that to your children. If you have something critical going on at your business and you must answer a message, tell your kid to hang on a moment. Finish what you're doing, shut down your phone or laptop, and turn your attention to your child. Children want to see your eyes. How many times has your child said, "Hey Dad, watch this!"?

If you're sleeping eight hours a night and working eight hours a day, that leaves just eight hours for everything else. In reality, you're probably putting in more than eight hours in the office, plus a couple more hours at home online. Use the time you have left wisely. It will make you and your loved ones happier, and you can return to work with no regrets or nagging feeling that you screwed up another evening at home. Because you cannot—I repeat, *cannot*—make that time up.

If you have a home office, as in "office in your home," establish working hours and communicate them to your family. Close the door during those hours if you have to. Teach your family to respect your work hours, then reciprocate by respecting the time they give to you by being totally present.

THREE POINTERS FOR MANAGING DISTRACTIONS

1. TIME BLOCKING

Find a calendar system you like, such as Google Calendar or even a day planner, and block out time for the most important activities. Include time with your family and time at work. If you play video games with one of your children for half an hour every evening, put it on your calendar. Make sure to block time for meals, commuting, and downtime too, for decompressing. You can even color-code activities and make them repeating to save time. Respect those times and don't let interruptions keep you from accomplishing whatever you have planned for those times. Once you've finished the goal or event, or when the time is up, you can delete it from your calendar and enjoy a divine sense of accomplishment. If an activity or event is important to you, prove it by putting it on your calendar.

Some people don't like blocking time out on their calendars. They prefer to work off a list of priorities, and that's fine too. If that method works for you, keep doing it. But at the end of the day, plug those accomplishments into your calendar so you have some kind of a record of what you did, and use it as a model for future days.

One day a week, say at the end of the day on Friday or Sunday night, review your calendar. See what you got done and what's left to do. Plan the upcoming week. Otherwise, your time will be filled with nonessential work and distractions. You could also end up saying yes to things you don't really want to do, because you don't have a solid reason for saying no. A time-blocked calendar gives you lots of reasons to turn down unnecessary activities.

As the late Stephen Covey noted, "The way to have the courage to say no to good ideas is by having a greater 'yes' burning inside." Covey's work emphasizes the importance of prioritizing one's values and goals to effectively manage time and make decisions.[24] Trust me, if my calendar has "Son's Football Practice" blocked in from 5:30 to 7:30 p.m., I will not be hanging around the office answering emails.

2. PHONE MANAGEMENT

Put your phone away. It's not a lifeline, and you won't die if you don't look at it every five minutes. During certain times of the day, such as when you're doing deep work, having dinner at home, or out with clients, put it out of sight. There's nothing more annoying than having lunch with someone whose phone is face up on the table, and the person is constantly looking at it instead of paying attention to you. Some people have "no cell phone" and "no online" rules for certain hours in their homes, not just for themselves but the whole family. Some people designate an entire day every week, usually a Sunday, as a "no tech" day. If you're running a business, you may not be able to disconnect completely, but you can take a few hours off in the evening, on weekends, and if you go on a vacation.

3. INFORM PEOPLE OF YOUR AVAILABILITY

Tell people your schedule, and let them know when you are available to them and when you are not to be interrupted. One thing you can do is instruct your staff to keep an ongoing list of items they want to talk to you about, and give them a time each day or each week to meet with you and discuss all the items on the list. This way, you avoid multiple distractions throughout the day, and you can tackle everything

---

24 Covey, *7 Habits*.

together all at once. In the meantime, odds are the employee will answer their questions and solve some of those problems themselves.

Sometimes I forget my own rules, and I usually regret it. One of my employees was supposed to pay a bill, and he hadn't paid it. I had sort of forgotten about it, but we had a weekly meeting scheduled, and I planned to ask him about it then. Before that meeting, I decided to just send him a quick text in the middle of the day. It wasn't a "Hey, you owe me money" kind of text, but more of a "Did you get the invoice I sent you?" text. He responded that he had received it, but he was at the hospital with his father-in-law and would take care of it as soon as he got back to the office. As you can imagine, I felt like a real jerk. Why couldn't I have waited for our scheduled weekly meeting?

Planning time with staff helps you manage your time, and it allows them to manage theirs as well. This goes for family members too. Plan regular times with them, and show up. One of my sons likes golf and cars. Another son likes video games, and he knows I'm good for two games with him every night. If I'm out of town for a few days, which is unavoidable, we get together that first evening I'm back to catch up. That's important. Coming home and then scheduling a night out with friends and colleagues would be, for me, a mistake.

Remember, as a parent, you're a role model for your kids. As a business owner, you're a role model for your staff. Show them how you want to be treated and how they should teach others to treat them. Don't be surprised if they create their own calendars and start blocking off time to spend with you.

Netflix was one of the first companies to introduce unlimited paid time off (PTO) for employees.[25] I wondered if I could do the same with my pest control company. Allowing people this freedom would be a huge benefit, I thought, because they could take time off when they needed it, without feeling as if they had to plan months in advance or feel guilty about it. My only worry was that they might take too much time off, but they were good people, and I didn't think

25   Reed Hastings and Erin Meyer, *No Rules Rules: Netflix and the Culture of Reinvention* (Penguin, 2020).

they'd abuse the new policy. Well, I got the opposite response. People took fewer days off. I learned that unless management modeled taking PTO, employees were afraid to take advantage of time off. So I had to take days off and instruct the managers to do the same to show the staff that we really wanted them to enjoy unlimited PTO and they would not be punished for it.

Again, modeling this behavior matters. Your staff shouldn't think they have to respond to every email or text message within two minutes. If they do, how will they get any deep work done?

Another common distraction is the "reply all" function in email. When you do that, expect every person to read the email, looking for why they were copied on it. What a waste of people's time—time you are paying them for. Respond to and copy the people who need the information. If you do hit reply all, check the list of people you're emailing. Unless you started the email thread, you don't know whose inbox you're going to land in. Remove anyone who doesn't need the information before hitting send. Otherwise, you are being the distraction.

PACK YOUR LUNCH AND AVOID "FAST FOOD" DISTRACTIONS

Entrepreneurs are easily distracted, chasing one business idea after another. We have to focus on one at a time and get it to the point that it can grow without our help. We're also interrupted by people and technology, and we need to protect ourselves from those distractions so we can focus on the hard, deep work that's important but not urgent.

Setting boundaries around your most important tasks protects them from technology, people, and other distractions. Entrepreneurs have to set boundaries for themselves too. A binder full of ideas is not the way to build a successful business. But if you can pull just one good idea from that binder and develop it, you will have a business. Like I told the young man who sat in my office that day, put the binder on a high shelf and don't look at it again until your first business is thriving without your day-to-day involvement. When you can take a month off and the business is still making money, still growing, then you can take the binder down and thumb through it, looking for the next good idea.

When I sat down to write this book, I wasn't sure which book to write. I had many book ideas. Maybe not a binder full, but enough to keep me writing for the rest of my life. I had to zero in on one—the one I thought would be most helpful to new entrepreneurs. The idea and message that wasn't getting out there. The solution to a problem that causes many new business owners to fail. If I had allowed myself to be distracted by all my other ideas, this book would be nothing more than an idea sitting on a shelf, unwritten. Putting all those other ideas aside allowed me the focus to finish this one. I'll get to the others, but for now, I have a book that can do its job and continue doing it without me. That was the goal I had for this book, and it's the kind of goal you need for your business.

Reframing small sacrifices as investments toward something greater applies to all areas of your life. This applies to distractions too. If you put aside the innate desire to pursue many businesses for a few years and focus on one, you'll create an amazing resource in that one company, which is what I did with my pest control business. It allowed me to fund the next business, and the next. I applied everything I learned from that business to the others, so launching them went more quickly. I would not have gotten to that point if I had been spreading my attention across multiple ventures. That singular focus was necessary to build my second, third, and my twentieth businesses, and I continue building on it today. In the meantime, I'm still working on avoiding all the other distractions that take time away from what really matters—family, friends, spirituality, and health. After all these years and all these businesses, I am still a work in progress.

PACK YOUR LUNCH QUESTIONS AND ACTIONS

1. If you showed me your calendar, would I be able to see what is important in your life?
2. What are the distractions you struggle with the most?
3. Has having too many business ideas prevented you from starting a business?
4. Do you enjoy envisioning what "might be" more than spending time executing on it?

7

YOUR LIFE WILL HAVE CONFLICT

"The only way to avoid conflict is to say nothing, do nothing, and be nothing."

—ARISTOTLE

Successful business owners seem to live blessed lives. They appear happy, or at least content and self-assured. Some of the feistier ones might trade barbs online and in interviews, but you don't see them engaging in knock-down, drag-out fights. For all the responsibility they carry, business owners' lives seem relatively calm.

Don't believe it. Running a business is loaded with conflicts, professional and personal. Experienced entrepreneurs have just learned to project a professional exterior and spend their time focusing on what they can control. They know that investors, employees, and customers are watching, and they can't come off as angry, confused, or conflicted leaders. What would that say about their businesses?

The Apple versus Microsoft rivalry began as a cooperative relationship but evolved into a fierce competition. Steve Jobs criticized Microsoft's lack of creativity and Bill Gates saving Apple from bankruptcy with a $150 million investment in 1997. Both companies have consistently clashed over technology innovation, from Graphic User Interface development to modern product lines like laptops and mobile devices. Despite their differences, their competition has driven significant technological advancements and shaped the personal computing and smartphone markets.[26]

For the past ten years, Uber and taxis have competed for dominance, but the rivalry is shifting as taxi fleets integrate into Uber's platform. Uber and taxi drivers working together benefits both parties. Taxi drivers gain access to increased earnings and customers through Uber, while Uber expands its supply and reduces costs, maintaining profitability.[27]

The hotel industry is undergoing significant transformation due to new technologies and competition from Airbnb, which has disrupted traditional models by impacting both supply and demand. Despite the challenges, technology presents opportunities for hotels to create better guest experiences, optimize operations, and improve profitability, which can offer the upper hand over Airbnb.[28] And the ultimate winner is the guest, who now has access to multiple hospitality options.

When I talk to people thinking of launching a business, I ask them who's supporting them. Who in their circle has their back? Almost without exception, they claim everyone supports them. Their family is behind them. Their business partners are their best friends. And though they don't have any employees or customers yet, they're certain those people won't cause any problems.

That's what I thought too. But the more I talked about my plans, the more pushback I got, and from the strangest places. My own father thought law school was a much better path for me than entre-

26   Anna Domanska, "Apple vs. Microsoft: The Real History," *Industry Leaders*, December 4, 2019, https://www.industryleadersmagazine.com/apple-vs-microsoft-the-real-history/.

27   Andrew J. Hawkins, "How Uber Learned to Stop Fighting and Play Nice with Taxis," *The Verge*, September 26, 2023, https://www.theverge.com/2023/9/26/23888950/uber-taxi-driver-referral-third-party-los-angeles.

28   Erika Weber, "How Airbnb Has Disrupted Hotel Management," Verdant, November 14, 2022, https://verdant.copeland.com/blog/how-airbnb-has-disrupted-hotel-management/.

preneurship. Some of my partners worked out, but I had to part ways with others. I've had difficult employees, impossible customers, and vengeful competition. I've also had awesome partners, staff, and clients, and some of my fiercest competition have become my greatest allies. Over the years, I've gotten so used to the conflicts that I've kind of forgotten about all the conflicts I dealt with early on. As I sit here writing this chapter, I am reminded of a lot of them that I've moved on from.

You won't always see the conflicts coming, but come they will. People you thought were your biggest supporters will become your biggest haters. If you're lucky, they'll just ignore you. They might badmouth you. They could even sue you. It happens. On the other hand, people who hated you because you took market share from them could become your colleagues, and you'll find ways to help each other succeed.

Business breeds conflict. It generates money and loses it. Business creates heroes and villains, successes and failures. It's emotional. And no matter how hard you try, business will create conflicts for you on the job and other places too. Conflict isn't inherently bad. How you respond to conflict determines whether it benefits or hurts your business.

Business breeds conflict.

LEARNING TO MANAGE CONFLICT

When I was younger, I didn't always handle conflicts well. I'd disagree with a partner or an employee and distance myself from them, sometimes ending the business relationship completely. These are some of my biggest failures in business.

In hindsight, I realized how immature and shortsighted that behavior was. I lost the opportunity to listen to what they were saying and try to see the matter from a different perspective. I might have learned something about my business because when people are complaining, they're often giving you valuable information that you don't see from your own point of view. I also ended relationships that could have proved very valuable in future business dealings.

I can't change the past, but I regret some of my actions, and I'm committed to learning from my mistakes. When I sense a conflict, instead of backing away, I lean in and make a point of listening to the differences. What is the person telling me that's causing me to become defensive? Is there a nugget of truth in what they're saying—something I'm not aware of and am maybe trying to avoid? This isn't to say that people I disagree with are always right. But they have a perspective about the way I manage my business, and they deserve my attention—not immediate rejection of their opinion, and especially not an automatic dismissal of our relationship.

This is what happens when you let emotions get in the way. In some ways, your business is like your children, and you take everything people say about it personally.

Occasionally, people do say things to push your buttons, but those times are rare. More often, people complain when their expectations aren't met and they feel shortchanged. Customers complain when they don't get what they paid for; employees complain when job satisfaction is low. Their complaints aren't meant to upset you. They're simply trying to state their case and defend it with the facts as they see them.

I was getting a lot of complaints about one particular technician. One after another, customers called to complain that he never showed up. "I waited and waited," they said, "and I swear, he never showed!" I checked my invoices and saw the tech had filed them for every job. My immediate thought was "Oh, these people must have missed him, or they weren't really home and they wanted to make sure he actually did the job. Whatever. Some customers just like to complain. But why so many, and for this one technician?" I was on my way to Las Vegas for a short vacation with my wife, and I was sort of irritated. But as the business owner, I couldn't ignore these calls. Were they a red flag that needed further investigation?

Sort of begrudgingly (remember, I was on vacation), I checked the GPS data on the technician's service vehicle. Holy moly, he had done the last eight jobs...from his apartment! So this guy was sitting in his apartment filing invoices. Nice. I had to fire him, apologize to those customers, and send out another technician.

It's hard not to get attached to your staff and believe they can do no wrong. My first instinct had been to defend the technician. The lesson there was not to let my emotions get in the way of my responses to complaints. I care about my staff and my customers, but sometimes they make mistakes. They don't always tell the truth. I assume the best about all of them, but I have to be open to the fact that they are human. And so I don't blindly defend an employee or a customer against the other without some investigation. I try to see their opinions from their perspectives before taking action.

When you get a complaint from a customer or an employee, stay neutral. Don't be defensive or take one side against the other, but express concern. Let the person know you care and that you will look into the matter and get back to them. As human beings, we all want to feel listened to. People want to know that someone is going to do something about their complaint, and as the business owner, that someone is you. Then do some digging. Uncover the facts before taking action. There was a good chance that the technician had done all those jobs. Other than the phone calls, I had no reason to believe he hadn't. But after that incident, I required all my technicians to take photos at their locations as proof of the work done.

CUSTOMER COMPLAINTS HAVE CHANGED AND SO HAVE CONFLICTS

Complaints used to be between a business owner or manager and a customer. Now people can leave reviews on sites like Google, and so the complaints and, more importantly, the responses can cause real damage to a company. The worst ones can go viral.

We've reached this plateau of "normal complaining" where we expect companies to have a mix of good and bad reviews, so we look for the outliers—serious complaints about horrible products and services, and totally inappropriate responses by the company.

I was shopping online for quick-drying fly-fishing pants, and I brought up all the worst ratings. Almost all the bad reviews were from people who had bought the pants in the past and weren't happy with the new, redesigned version. I read their comments about what had changed, and they still sounded like pants I would like. I also read the responses from the company, which were excellent. Unhappy customers were politely told that the company had a money-back guarantee. They were provided with instructions and a link to the return process. That way, even customers who weren't happy with the pants came away with a positive experience.

Technology, the internet, and sites like Google have given everyone a megaphone for airing their grievances. They've also provided business owners with a megaphone for blasting their awesomeness. We can do this with outstanding customer relations, witnessed by our responses to the good reviews and the bad ones.

I'm actually leery of businesses with all five-star reviews. A few bad ones give the reviewers more credibility so I don't question whether the business owner paid their employees to leave good reviews. I welcome an occasional poor review because it informs me of something I could do better, gives me the opportunity to make things right with the customer and perhaps even encourage repeat business, and gives me the chance to show off how accommodating and responsive I am and how much I value customers and their feedback. Where else do you get a chance to do all that, and for free no less?

That opportunity is especially important for businesses that sell services on online platforms, like my pest control business. There's no storefront, and so a customer can't just walk in and tell me what they think. There's no product to write a review about. The interaction between company and client is limited. The company—and its prospective clients—can go online and see what other people are saying, though.

EXPECT MORE CRITICISM THAN PRAISE

After a flight from Detroit to Myrtle Beach, as the plane taxied toward the terminal, the flight attendant came over the loudspeaker and noted, half-jokingly, "Be sure to tell all your friends that your pilot got you to your destination early today. Because we know that if you were late, you would tell everybody!" She was right. People tend to focus on the negatives and ignore all the positive experiences they have with products and services. It's up to you, the business owner, to welcome their feedback, good and bad, so they feel comfortable sharing it with you and getting a resolution instead of complaining to anyone who will listen (on their social media pages, in reviews, at work, in line at the grocery store...) what a horrible job Company X did for them. Likewise, respond to their good reviews—a simple thank-you will do—so they're more inclined to continue praising you.

CONFLICTS WITH EMPLOYEES

This attitude of being open to criticism and praise works just as well with employees. If you ask an employee how they feel about their position and how it might be improved, they should feel comfortable giving you an honest response and not worry about retaliation. Often your employees are the closest people to your customers and their problems. They can also be a great source for solutions. Take advantage of what they know and are learning day-to-day on the job. Don't discount it, and if they have suggestions for making their jobs better so they can make your business better and your customers happier, listen. They have a different perspective from yours and are spending many more hours in the business, not on the business like you are.

CONFLICTS WITH COMPETITORS

Competitors may ignore you. Then again, if you're really impacting their business, they may come after you with bad (fake) reviews. Occasionally a competitor goes beyond the normal range of behavior to, well, slightly *de*ranged. There was a guy who called our Long Island, New York, pest control office, for example, pretending to be a cop. He said if we didn't stop selling our services door-to-door, he'd show up at our office. We sort of ignored him, so he called back and said he was with the mob. He physically threatened some of the staff members. It turned out that he owned a competing pest control company, and we were taking some of his customers! That kind of competitor doesn't turn up often, thankfully, but if they do, you have to deal with them promptly. Like, get the actual police involved because you don't know what someone like that might do. They could be harmless, but then again, you don't want to put your staff at risk.

CONFLICTS WITH FAMILY AND FRIENDS

If your business fails, people will talk about you. If it succeeds, they'll talk about you. But probably not nearly as often as you might think. There's a saying credited to Olin Miller (among others, but he said it back in 1936) that goes, "You probably wouldn't worry about what people think of you if you could know how seldom they do."

Still, some will talk, and it won't always be pleasant. If your business is going well, they'll be jealous of the time it takes away from your relationship with them, or the fact that you proved them wrong, or that you did it at all, while they're still stuck in a job they hate. If your business falters, they'll remind you that you should have listened to them and not even tried in the first place because, you know, "You don't have what it takes to be an entrepreneur." I got wind of people saying that all I cared about was money, and if I was a better husband, I would spend more time at home. This affected me deeply. But those people didn't see the entire picture. As an entrepreneur, you'll be putting in more time initially, but with a plan to work less so you can spend more time on relationships, hobbies, and of course, launching your next business!

Eventually, some of those people who created conflict in your life will come around. In the words of Nicholas Klein, "First they ignore you. Then they ridicule you. And then they attack you and want to burn you. And then they build monuments to you."[29] Are there monuments in your future? That is up to you.

Being a business owner can turn you into a very self-centered person. I've been there. I had to train myself to turn my thoughts outward instead of inward and ask myself, "What's going on in the rest of the world? What's going on with the people I care most about?"

This is one reason I started the nonprofit Proof Gives Back through my pest control company. The time I spent in a third-world country never left my heart, and I'm fully aware of how lucky I am to live where I live and enjoy everything our country has to offer. Nothing makes you count your blessings more than seeing the struggles of others. There are those who have more, sure, but there are many more with much less. There's a saying that goes something like "If the world threw their problems into a pile, and we got to select which ones we'd pull out, a lot of us would choose our own."

It's tough to get all worked up over a bad day at work when you realize how many people don't have running water (more than two million in the US alone)[30] or how many kids live in homes with insufficient food (more than fourteen million in the US).[31]

Remember, as a business owner, you will be making short-term sacrifices to enjoy long-term freedom and success. Those short-term sacrifices do not involve giving up food and running water. In the big scheme of things, as they say, you are not giving up that much.

29   Attributed to Nicholas Klein. Originates from a speech delivered by the labor union advocate in May 1918 during an address to the Amalgamated Clothing Workers of America during their biennial convention in Baltimore.

30   George McGraw and Radhika Fox, *Closing the Water Access Gap in the United States: A National Action Plan* (Dig Deep and US Water Alliance, 2019), https://www.digdeep.org/close-the-water-gap.

31   "Facts About Child Hunger in America," No Kid Hungry, accessed November 27, 2024, https://www.nokidhungry.org/who-we-are/hunger-facts.

Just make sure you don't sacrifice the wrong things, or you'll be left with regret.

REMEMBER WHY YOU ARE DOING THIS

When you feel conflict coming on, resist the urge to react. Step back and remind yourself why you started a business. Was it to be miserable—and miserable to be around—every day? Or was it to have more freedom to live life your way? Then ask yourself, "How do my responses move me forward in that direction (and not the other one)?"

Recall your motivation. Lean into it. This works for conflicts at work and in personal relationships, by the way. If your kids are trying your last nerve, remind yourself why you started a family in the first place. If your spouse is bugging you, think back to when you first met. Without those people in your life, what would being a business owner be like? For most people, it would be much less fulfilling. You need people to share your life with—the failures, successes, and everything in between. And they need you too.

James Lawrence, a.k.a. the Iron Cowboy, finished fifty triathlons in fifty states in fifty consecutive days. Crazy, huh? Years ago, he was the guest speaker at my company's summer kickoff. I asked him if what he had sacrificed to accomplish this feat was worth it. He said that he was probably doing harm to his body, but there was something bigger he was after. For him, the sacrifice paid off.

No matter how well you prepare, conflict is inevitable for business owners. How you respond to conflict determines the outcome. As you weigh sacrifices, aim for a net positive result. Make sure that what you are getting from the sacrifice is greater in the long run than what you give up in the short term. Revisit your life's categories, and never put your core relationships and other priorities at risk.

If you're feeling the stress from work, find a way to decompress instead of taking the pressure home with you. Sometimes the commute home is enough to separate work conflict from home life, but with many people working from home, that isn't always an option.

While working from home offers significant advantages, such as eliminating the daily commute and improving work/life balance, a recent study suggests that commuting serves as a crucial transition period that helps individuals mentally detach from work and reduces stress, implying that some form of routine to mark the end of the workday is beneficial, even for remote workers.[32]

Go to the gym after work or out for a run. Take a cold plunge or sit in the sauna. This isn't just about protecting relationships with people at home; it's also about your own physical and mental health. You need a break from conflicts. If you're brooding over something that happened hours ago, you're not resting and recovering. You might as well be at work, because that's where your mind and emotions are. If you commute to work, use the time on the train or subway to read or catch up on a favorite podcast. Meditate. Separate yourself from the demands of work and prepare your mind for relaxation (i.e., psychologically detach). If you drive, listening to music can keep you in the moment instead of dwelling on the past and worrying about the future. The goal is to lower the intensity that's required of you as a business owner, especially a new one. You have to turn it down a few notches—or a lot of notches—or you'll burn out.

USE CONFLICT TO IMPROVE

Conflict has a negative connotation, often rightfully so. It's uncomfortable, it's awkward, and it can change relationships. However, viewed objectively, conflict can benefit your business.

Shift your mindset to accept conflict, seek the granules of truth in it, and use them to get better. This requires introspection—considering what you believe, why you believe it, and whether the conflict provides evidence that could change your beliefs.

---

32 Léa Drouelle, "Could Work Commutes Actually Help Us Mentally Decompress?" ETX Daily Up, February 10, 2023, https://dailyup.etxstudio.com/articles/rn/en/news_206Dr5Kg/psychology/could-work-commutes-actually-help-us-mentally-decompress.

Very few conflicts are as significant as they first appear, and much of conflict is a learning experience. Even the conflicts that seem ominous don't have to be. Decide how much importance you're going to place on them, and pick your battles wisely. If a customer lies outright in a review, should you call them a liar? Probably not, because even though you're right, you'll come across badly. Respond politely and do what you can to resolve the misunderstanding.

Consider how the conflict and your response to it affects you, your business, and your priorities. Responding rationally and without the automatic emotions you're feeling is a learned skill, so don't expect to be good at it right away. With practice, you'll get better. Much of this comes with age and wisdom.

A while back, I flew to San Diego to record on a fairly popular podcast. Then I waited for it to air. The host never aired it. I can't tell you how much that bothered me! I drove myself a little nuts worrying and wondering about that podcast. Did I do a good enough job? Did the host not like me? Did he forget about it or accidentally erase it? I will never know, and I'll never get back the time I wasted thinking about it. That's what happens when you dwell on conflicts, internal and external. The energy wasted can do more damage than the actual conflict.

Acknowledge and accept that there will be conflict. Have faith in yourself to resist reacting to it. Instead, learn from it and respond appropriately. Never lose sight of your priorities, and ensure your responses to conflict don't affect them. Over time, you'll gain the wisdom to deal with conflict better and better, learning from your responses and mistakes and from the outcomes. This will serve you and your business in the long run.

PACK YOUR LUNCH QUESTIONS AND ACTIONS

1. When a conflict appears, is your natural reaction fight or flight?
2. Are there people in your life that you experience regular conflict with?

3. What practices have you used to avoid emotional responses to conflict scenarios?

4. Are you able to identify any benefits that come from conflict?

8

YOUR STRESS
WILL INCREASE

"Stress should be a powerful driving force, not an obstacle."

—BILL PHILLIPS

Four or five months into starting Proof, I was incredibly stressed out and unhappy. I had moved my family to the Detroit suburbs, and nothing seemed to be going right. That's probably an exaggeration, but as a typical entrepreneur, I'm naturally hard on myself. When I don't see immediate results, I worry. Those people who walk around the block every day and pat themselves on the back? I'm not one of them. Some days I wish I were. I'm a guy who is never satisfied. Thankful? Sure. But satisfied? Never.

I overlook my accomplishments and focus on what I haven't done. That mindset has been a curse and a blessing, driving me to succeed but making the process less than pleasant. I've become a lot better, though, but I had to learn to be intentional about celebrating those successes. In the meantime, I went through some very stressful periods.

The first really stressful time caught me by surprise. I expected that being a business owner would be less stressful than answering to a boss every day. I also expected instant success. The fact was that Proof had scaled quickly. We had quite a few employees and customers. In fact, we grew more in our first five months in business than most companies grow within their first five years! You'd think I'd be jumping for joy.

But there was difficulty between my brother and me, between my wife and my brother, between me and my wife... Then there were the vendors, employees, and customers who, as much as I appreciated them, were like so many distractions vying for attention. I wasn't used to spreading myself so thin and didn't know how to handle it. Eventually I figured out the problem, which was failing to incorporate two critical components into my life: I didn't have boundaries to protect myself from stress, and I didn't have outlets to relieve whatever stress I couldn't avoid. That oversight had a snowball effect, compounding and bearing down on me. Stress led to stress eating. It led to working more hours, spending less time with my family, and getting less sleep—all of which created more stress.

I don't remember whose idea it was—mine or my wife's—but at a point, the two of us started going to the gym. This wasn't a foreign place to me because I went to the gym during high school. I'd always played sports too, especially basketball, not so much for exercise as for recreation. It has been ten years since we started going to the gym, and now I can't imagine life without it. Working out in an environment away from home, work, and all the technological connections to those places puts you in a different headspace immediately.

Okay, confession time: at first, I was one of those guys who brought my work to the gym, carrying my cell phone around and answering text messages while I worked out. Unless you're an on-call emergency doc or firefighter, there is no excuse for that kind of behavior. Even the president of the United States takes a break now and then (golf, anyone?), and the Secret Service doesn't interrupt them unless it's *really* important. Are you the president of the United States? Doctor or firefighter? Me neither, so we get actual uninterrupted breaks. During those times, you don't stop thinking about your business and worrying about your clients completely, but you do it from a less stressful, often more creative perspective. You're not in problem-solving mode. Sometimes that is exactly *when* the solution to an issue becomes clear—when you aren't trying to solve it.

For me, the daily exercise also had a compounding effect. I started eating healthier, for one. I slept better too. But I had to do more. I wasn't in control of my schedule and was leading a reactionary existence, constantly putting out fires and spending more time working in the business than on the business. Once my stress simmered down, I could think more clearly. It became clear that I had to set boundaries to guard against stress in the first place.

I remember when I realized something had to change. Sitting in my office at six o'clock in the evening after everyone else had gone home, I was looking over my to-do list and feeling like a failure. I had been there all day, yet it seemed as if I had accomplished very little. There was so much more to do. Feeling miserable and not wanting to take those feelings home with me, I completed a few to-dos and called it a day. At home, my wife mentioned how unhappy I seemed. She was right. We talked about happiness and how it wasn't an accident or fate that brought us happiness. We had some control, if only we exerted it. I made the decision right then and there to make whatever changes were necessary to put me on the path toward a happier life. That meant identifying whatever was causing my stress and doing something about it. Controlling your time and resources alleviates stress. When you're in control, you decide how to spend your time and what tasks to ignore. You don't let other people dictate your schedule.

Stress sneaks up on you. One minute life is peachy, and the next you feel like your head's in a vise and you're struggling to decide your next move. You have so much to do and don't know where to start, so you do busywork. Or you do nothing at all. Neither option fixes the problem. They only make it worse.

CAUSES OF STRESS

When you start a business, your stress increases for several reasons. You're at the top of the company, and there's no one to hand off the biggest problems to. Like they say, "the buck stops with you." You can't tap out and wait for someone else to do the hard work. You can't leave your troubles behind and go on vacation. It's your business, and the most difficult problems to solve are your main responsibility.

Your business will feel personal to you—much more personal than a job where you work for someone else. So the problems feel personal.

You interact with employees, customers, vendors, the bank, and other businesses, and relationships with these people can cause stress. They are all looking to you for something—good work, a paycheck, products and services—and it's your responsibility to ensure they get it.

Then there's the infrastructure, physical and online. Is your building safe and clean? How's your website looking? If you have a fleet of vehicles, are they maintained?

EMPLOYEE STRESS

Employees are people, and so, like most people, they want to do a good job for you. But some people can cause serious problems. Before sending a technician to someone's home for bedbug service, I provide the customer with a checklist to prepare the property. They're instructed to open all the furniture drawers in the rooms being treated to ensure thorough coverage. One time, a technician poked around in a drawer and stole an envelope of cash. It belonged to a kid in college who was saving money for a car. There were thousands of dollars involved, and the tech went to jail for that. In the meantime, I was stressed out about the situation, the customer, and what the incident would do to my company's reputation.

These days, people have cameras in front of their homes and in their houses. You would think anyone providing an in-home service would be aware of this and be on their best behavior. That's not always the case. I've spoken to other business owners who've had even more serious problems with employees behaving inappropriately on customers' property, and it's a real concern. This is why vetting and hiring people is so critical, especially customer-facing employees who can do real damage to your business.

With so many moving parts, you expect certain things to go wrong. You could run out of materials. Customers could cancel appointments or not show up. Employees will be late or quit. But so much can go wrong that you don't expect, and responding to the surprises is stressful.

Though you won't know everything that can happen ahead of time, you can identify situations that would cause the most stress and do your best to avoid them at all costs. I've had colleagues who were short on payroll. Not being able to pay employees is one of the worst things you can do. It's not only stressful for you; it causes incredible stress for the people relying on that money to pay their bills. If I were to list the nonnegotiables in my business, that would be at the top of the list. It's not acceptable to expect people to work for you if you aren't prepared to pay them.

Employee safety is also at the top, followed closely by customer satisfaction. Here, it's important to set reasonable expectations with your customer and make sure you meet or exceed them. However, don't stretch yourself so thin making them happy that you make yourself miserable in the process.

When I worked as an attorney, I represented a large credit card company that had many small cases against people who didn't make their payments. Preparing for one of these trials, I worried that the client hadn't sent me any supporting documents. I didn't have a witness either. I read the disclosures from the other attorneys, and knew I was in trouble. How could I possibly win the case? How could the client expect me to stand in front of a judge and the opposing party's counsel with absolutely no evidence to support my side of the case?

I stormed into my boss's office, livid over the situation the card company had put me in. He leaned back in his chair with his hands behind his head, fingers interlocked, with the ease of a man who has had this conversation many times before. He said, "Allan, you can't care more about their case than they do." *Mic drop*. He explained that the credit card company had thousands of cases like this one, and they didn't expect to win them all. They litigated them anyway to send the message that people couldn't just charge up their cards and not pay them off without consequences. If that became the norm, the company would be out of business. In fact, they lost money on these cases because they had to pay attorneys, but the cost outweighed the potential cost of allowing people to take advantage of their credit.

Since then, I have employed that lesson—I can't care more than they do—innumerable times. And though I put customer satisfaction near the top of my nonnegotiables, I keep in mind that meeting expectations is necessary, and exceeding them is better, but stressing myself out to deliver products and services the customer doesn't care about is not worth my time.

SELF-IMPOSED STRESS

Most of our stress as business owners comes from ourselves. Highly motivated people can struggle to live up to their own expectations. Sound familiar? No matter how much we accomplish, in our minds, it's never enough. In the book *The Gap and the Gain*, Dan Sullivan notes the advantages of focusing on the *gain* between where we are now versus where we used to be; in other words, our progress. The *gap*, which he persuades us to avoid, is our focus on the distance between where we are now and where we want to be.[33]

Stress impacts us mentally and emotionally. We become frustrated, agitated, and short on patience not only with the cause of the stress, but with the people and other activities in which we engage. When I have a tough morning and my wife calls to see if I'd like to go out that

---

33   Dan Sullivan and Benjamin Hardy, *The Gap and the Gain: The High Achievers' Guide to Happiness, Confidence, and Success* (Hay House, 2021).

evening and I say no, what am I saying no to? Am I responding to her or to the stress? She knows me well enough that when I respond that way, she'll ask why. That's my cue to examine my response—which was likely a reaction—and make a better decision. Of course I want to go out with my wife! Those stressful moments can linger long into the day, though, coloring our reactions and decisions that have nothing to do with the problem at hand.

Do you ever feel kind of off, like something's wrong, but you can't put your finger on it? It may be due to a stressful situation you encountered earlier in the day and forgot about, but the feelings have stuck with you. Likewise, you might be in a terrific mood, seemingly for no particular reason, but maybe you got some great news earlier that day and, hours later, it slipped your mind. Yet those positive feelings linger.

GOOD STRESS VERSUS BAD STRESS

In the article "What Is Eustress? A Look at the Psychology and Benefits," psychologist Catherine Moore argues that by understanding and embracing eustress, or positive stress, individuals can transform their perception of stress from a harmful force into a source of motivation and resilience. Drawing on psychological research and the work of scholars like Kelly McGonigal, Moore explores how reframing stress as eustress can improve overall well-being, enhance performance, and foster a more balanced, fulfilling life, free from the debilitating effects of distress. Through practical applications and evidence-based strategies, the author aims to shift the narrative surrounding stress and unlock its potential for personal growth.[34]

Ultimately, it's not the situation that creates stress, but how you respond to it. When you allow challenges to motivate you toward positive actions and change, you experience eustress, which is a good stress. Reacting negatively to challenges creates bad stress, or distress.

---

34   Catherine Moore, "What Is Eustress? A Look at the Psychology and Benefits," Positive Psychology, November 13, 2024, https://positivepsychology.com/what-is-eustress/.

You have a choice. If a valued employee gives you two weeks' notice, you can accept the fact that no matter how good a business owner you are or how hard you've worked to satisfy your employees, people are still going to quit. Then you can take action to replace the person. That's good stress. Your other option is to waste time stewing over it, blaming the person or yourself, and fail to solve the problem. The end result? The bad kind of stress—*distress*. Remember, stress should be our friend, not our enemy.

Distress is demotivating. It makes us unproductive and emotionally unwell. Prolonged distress can make you feel like you aren't good at your job. You lose confidence. For a new business owner, the lines between eustress and distress get blurred. There's so much to do, and the feelings you experience of being overwhelmed might seem unnatural. I recall thinking to myself, "Is this normal?" Yes, it is normal, but you have to separate the good stress from the bad and learn to respond to challenges in a way that promotes eustress and keeps distress at bay.

During the first few months of launching a business, the stress is palpable. It's a shock to the system. You'll notice a change but won't know exactly what's different. You just don't feel good anymore. The feeling is especially intense if you've come out of a well-paying job at an established business in a reliable industry to start a business from scratch. Not to mention opening that business in another state, like I did.

Leading up to the actual launch, you lay the foundation. This includes activities like organizing your LLC, opening a business checking account, building a website, and getting your marketing lined up. You feel busy, and you're discovering new territory, but that time is fairly mellow.

There's a point when everything changes. The internal pressures you put on yourself don't go away, but now they're joined by external pressures. You quit your job, and with no income coming in, you still have bills to pay. You open the doors to your business, and customers want something from you. And then your employees want to be paid. The problems change, and they are often problems you've never encountered.

If you scale quickly, the pressure increases just as quickly. In time, it levels off, but for a while it's like drinking from a fire hose, and you wonder if the pressure will ever lighten up.

Any change in your business—positive or negative—adds stress. This includes adding employees and employees quitting, getting new customers and losing them, and making more or less money. Growing your business or changing in any way affects the acceleration and/or the direction, destabilizing the business in the short term. Entrepreneurs think growing their business will be easy. They don't consider that scaling a business doesn't mean just making more money. More business means more employees, more customers, and more work. For this reason, some people choose not to grow their business. That's a viable option. Just not one for people like me.

STRESS IS NECESSARY...BUT IT'S NOTHING TO BRAG ABOUT

As difficult as stress may seem, it's necessary to your growth as a business owner. Without challenges, there are no opportunities to try new things, learn, and improve. Without challenges, you are stuck in the status quo. You might reach a point where you are content with how big your business has become and decide to stay there. You'll have less stress, but you will also stagnate. That's a choice you can make. It's definitely a trade-off because at a point, you won't need to make more money. You won't want more stress in your life. You will want to divert your time to other things. That point could be one successful business or ten. It could be becoming a millionaire or a centimillionaire. It could be putting in forty hours or twenty hours a week on the business or stepping aside and hiring someone to run it for you.

Stress isn't unique to new business owners. It affects entrepreneurs at every stage, from people who are struggling to launch a business to those who appear to be at the top of their game. Some business leaders find ways to destress, while others continue to struggle.

- **Elon Musk**—Known for his work with companies like Tesla and SpaceX, Musk has openly talked about the immense stress and long hours he endures. He has mentioned experiencing sleep deprivation and physical exhaustion due to his intense work schedule and stress.[35]
- **Howard Schultz**—The former CEO of Starbucks has spoken about the stress of expanding Starbucks and the physical toll it took on him. He experienced chronic back pain and other stress-related health issues.[36]
- **Steve Jobs**—The tech visionary's love for walking was driven by its numerous benefits, including boosting creativity, reducing stress, and enhancing communication. He often held meetings and engaged in serious conversations while walking, believing it energized the brain and fostered innovative thinking. The scientific evidence supports these benefits, highlighting how walking can improve mood, health, and cognitive functions, making it a valuable practice for both personal and professional growth.[37]

35 Paul A. Eisenstein, "Elon Musk Recounts His 'Excruciating' Year, Admits to Taking Sleeping Pills, Working 120-Hour Weeks," *NBC News*, August 17, 2018, https://www.nbcnews.com/business/autos/elon-musk-recounts-his-excruciating-year-admits-taking-sleeping-pills-n901611.

36 Rebecca Morin, "Ex-Starbucks CEO Howard Schultz, Mulling a Run for President, Taking Summer Off After Back Surgeries," *USA Today*, June 12, 2019, https://www.usatoday.com/story/news/politics/elections/2019/06/12/former-starbucks-ceo-howard-schultz-recovering-from-back-surgeries/1435573001/.

37 Jonny Evans, "Here Is Why Apple's Steve Jobs Loved to Walk and So Should You," Apple Must, October 16, 2021, https://www.applemust.com/here-is-why-apples-steve-jobs-loved-to-walk-and-so-should-you/#google_vignette.

In time, you get better at handling stress. Your threshold for it increases. Situations that once stressed you out don't anymore. You probably lost sleep over the first customer that canceled, but now you understand that no business holds on to every customer forever. In time, if you end up with a particularly difficult customer, you might recommend they get their services elsewhere. I don't tolerate customers who are abusive to my employees, for example, and so if they can't be respectful, I let them know that we will no longer be working for them. Letting go of bad customers may be stressful in the short term, but in the long run your stress level will thank you.

We all know someone who's constantly complaining about how stressed out they are. They have more work and more problems than anyone else. They're not actually complaining though; they're kind of bragging, trying to convince people that they're more productive. Which is kind of ironic because they spend so much time talking about their stress that they have little time to do any real work.

Still, there's a cultural side to stress that's been around for many years where some people equate stress and productivity, and they equate productivity and value. So the more stressed they are, the more valuable they must be. Often, the most valuable people in the office don't talk about what they do at all. They're busy working. This isn't to say that complaints about stress should be ignored. If you have employees complaining about stress, you have to take them seriously and get to the root of the problem. They may be chronic complainers, but then again, they may have a real problem that needs your attention. In this case, you're in a position to help.

However, when it's you that's complaining (or bragging), don't expect anyone to step up to carry the burden. As the business owner, you have to help yourself. Instead of proclaiming yourself to be the hardest-working, most stressed-out person in the office, set boundaries that protect you from stress and then find ways to relieve it. Set those examples for your staff.

HOW STRESS IMPACTS YOUR
PHYSICAL AND MENTAL HEALTH

In their book *The 4 Disciplines of Execution*, authors Chris McChesney, Sean Covey, and Jim Huling note, "According to Dr. Ray Levey, founder of the Global Medical Forum, 80 percent of our health-care budget is consumed by five behavioral issues: Smoking, drinking, overeating, *stress*, and not enough exercise."[38] (The emphasis is mine.)

Chronic stress, resulting from modern-day demands such as work, family, and financial pressures, can continuously activate the body's natural stress response, leading to long-term health issues like anxiety, heart disease, and memory problems. Understanding and managing stress through healthy coping mechanisms, such as exercise, relaxation techniques, and professional counseling, is crucial for mitigating these risks and improving overall well-being.[39]

Your stress will increase. This is a sacrifice you must make to get your business off the ground in the short term. You will continue to experience stress in the long term, but protecting yourself from unnecessary stress and relieving the stress you can't avoid will allow you to survive the increased stress of business ownership. Learning to respond to stress appropriately can turn stress into eustress, a motivator, instead of distress, an inhibitor to business success.

Even as your stress level increases, don't accept high levels of it as normal. Do not try to convince yourself that the stress is acceptable because you are being productive. Over time, stress has damaging effects. Take your health into account and find ways to mitigate situations that cause you the most stress.

Stress often comes from situations that aren't important in the long run. In *The 7 Habits of Highly Effective People*, Stephen Covey notes that fitting big rocks, pebbles, and sand in a jar only works if you start with the big rocks and work your way down. If you start filling the

---

38 Chris McChesney et al., *The 4 Disciplines of Execution: Achieving Your Wildly Important Goals* (Free Press, 2012), 292.

39 Mayo Clinic Staff, "Chronic Stress Puts Your Health at Risk," Mayo Clinic, August 1, 2023, https://www.mayoclinic.org/healthy-lifestyle/stress-management/in-depth/stress-art-20046037.

jar first by adding sand, then pebbles, you will not have room for the big rocks.[40] It's the same with your business. Focus on the big rocks, and the pebbles and sand will take care of themselves.

Your biggest rocks are the priorities you identified within your life's categories. Within your business are other big rocks. Save your stress for those, and like they say, "don't sweat the small stuff."

This is easier said than done, but when we see other people focusing on matters of lesser importance, it seems obvious. You probably watched the series *Tiger King*, which aired on Netflix during COVID. The owner of an exotic animal zoo kept lions, tigers, and other dangerous creatures on his property. After a horrible accident where one of his employees suffered an injury so severe that he opted to have his arm amputated, proprietor Joseph "Joe Exotic" Maldonado remarked, "I'm never going to financially recover from this."[41]

Anyone watching that show saw immediately how inappropriate the comment was. We don't know whether Joe Exotic was focusing on matters of less importance or if his priorities were horribly out of whack. Regardless, you can see how obvious it is that getting stressed out about minor details is ridiculous, especially when someone just lost a body part.

Unchecked stress will impact you physically. It does not always manifest itself suddenly, and it can creep up on you. You might not even be conscious of it, but then one day you realize your shoulders have been sore for weeks.

I carry stress in my shoulders and neck. Sometimes I get a knot in the middle of my back. The discomfort isn't caused by a gym workout, which is a different kind of soreness. It's stress-related, usually due to doing too much for an extended period of time. If you compare yourself to a car, it's like holding the gas pedal down too long. It's okay

---

40   Covey, *7 Habits*.

41   Adrianna Freedman, "Here's What Happened to Kelci Saffery After *Tiger King*," *Men's Health*, March 25, 2020, https://www.menshealth.com/entertainment/a31926656/tiger-king-kelci-saffery-netflix/.

to hit it once in a while, maybe to pass someone on the freeway, but hold it too long and you will run into something.

Stress can affect your posture, which causes more physical problems. I didn't realize how my own posture was affected until a guy at the gym approached me and said, "I bet you work at a computer all day. I can tell by how your shoulders are hunched forward." Sure enough, when I looked in the mirror, I could see he was right. My posture had changed. After that, I became conscious of how I was sitting at my desk. Hunching my shoulders not only impacted my posture; it added to the stress on my body. I also noticed that when I was mentally stressed, I hunched even more! My workspace was ergonomically sound, but unless I intentionally sat upright with my butt and shoulders back, I was stressing my body.

Unless someone points the problem out to you, you may not be aware that your body's hurting. You get used to it, and you get used to seeing a person with poor posture in the mirror. I didn't realize how bad it was until I took measures to correct the problem with better seated posture and workouts at the gym. After a short time, I felt better. I believe the feeling is similar to putting on weight little by little. You don't notice the pounds adding up until they hinder your activities, and if you lose the weight, you get some or all of that functionality back. That's when you realize how much those pounds were limiting you.

Stress can cause serious physical problems, such as hair loss, migraines, high blood pressure, and even brain damage. I've gotten ocular migraines during periods of high stress. The first sign for me is blurred vision, and so now whenever I have the slightest problem seeing my computer screen, I nip the problem in the bud. Going into a dark room, closing my eyes, and practicing breath work prevents the symptoms from turning into a full-fledged, debilitating migraine. If you have symptoms like this, definitely see a doctor. It could very well be stress-related, or something else, but you can't run a business that way.

Stress manifests in many ways. Be aware of how you feel physically, mentally, and emotionally. Identify the symptoms of stress and get control of what's going on before it takes over. I can't overstate how important this is. I get it; we're all trying to run businesses. We don't have time for migraines, or high blood pressure, or worse. We'll just push through—one more hour, another day, and then we'll be fine. It doesn't work that way. For me, taking a few hours to head off a migraine was better than powering through the work only to be laid up for days. That was only the short-term impact. Prolonged negative stress will take years off your life, and no business is worth that kind of sacrifice.

Many entrepreneurs think they're as serious about their health as they are about their businesses. They don't drink or smoke. They work out, lift weights, eat right, and take vitamins every day. They monitor their weight and their sleep, do cold plunges, enjoy the sauna, and do everything else under the sun to stay healthy. Yet they allow stress to run rampant in their lives. But stress is like an invisible killer. It doesn't come in a six-pack or a Styrofoam tray. It just creeps up on you, silently picking away at your health and happiness.

PROTECTING YOURSELF FROM STRESS— PROACTIVE ACTIONS TO TAKE

In Chapter 6, we explored boundaries and why you have to protect your time from people and other distractions. This is critical to having time to run your business. It's imperative to maintaining peace of mind. Set boundaries for yourself, such as staying off social media, email, text messages, and your phone during a set time. Communicate those boundaries to people who may contact you so they know what to expect and respect your boundaries.

Otherwise, they will make their priorities yours when chances are those priorities aren't important to you or your business. I have a weekly catch-up call with my executive assistant, Tori, and unless the building's on fire, I don't allow emails, text messages, or phone calls to interrupt us. This ensures we have the time necessary to discuss whatever happened since our last meeting that needs our attention, and what's coming up that day, before diving into our day's work. My EA sets that time aside on her calendar, as do I, and we respect one another's time.

There's always that one person who knows you're not available and will still try every way possible to get your attention. This happened to me recently. A colleague called and texted continually to get my attention. I glanced at my phone to make sure nothing was on fire, and then I put it away and continued with the meeting. Sounds simple enough, but when you're new to business and you have new employees, new customers, and new partners, you feel the need to be on call for all of them 24/7. That's a sure path to getting none of the important work done, followed by burnout.

We do have to be there for all those people. But we also have to control the access they have to us so we can focus on our priorities and then give people our full attention within a reasonable time period. There's a saying that "you teach people how to treat you," and it's absolutely true when it comes to boundaries. If you respond right away to every high-maintenance person at your business, they will continue to hound you, always expecting an immediate response. The first time you wait ten minutes to respond, they'll freak out, thinking you're ignoring them. Set rules for yourself, such as responding to text messages within three hours (unless the building really is on fire), emails within twenty-four hours, and phone calls by the end of the day. These are suggestions, and you should come up with whatever you believe are reasonable response times.

Set contact methods and times for the different groups of people you interact with in your business. My family can call me anytime, and they know that. They also know that unless it's an emergency, I probably won't return their call right away. My EA can also call or text anytime, but she understands what warrants immediate action and what can be put off until our next scheduled meeting.

I do not give my personal cell phone number out to customers. But I do ensure they have plenty of opportunities to contact me in other ways during business hours. I model my preferred communication too. For example, if an employee calls me too often, I might start responding, after some time, with a text message. This is my way of telling them, "I'd prefer that you text me with these kinds of questions." Texting is quicker for me, and I can see at a glance if there's a problem that needs my attention. With a phone call, I have to answer the call or listen to the voicemail. Nine times out of ten, it could have waited.

Setting boundaries with employees is particularly important. Otherwise, they might try to involve you in problems that have nothing to do with the job. When you have complete freedom and your business is growing by leaps and bounds without you in the office every day, you might have time to take on other people's problems. As a new business owner, you do not. Establishing this kind of boundary can be tough for entrepreneurs because we're drawn to problems. It's not the problem but the opportunity to figure out a solution that pulls us in. We want to be helpful. It's in our nature.

When employees come to you with problems related to the business, you have to pay attention, but you don't have to solve the problem. Encourage people to consider several solutions and bring those to you so you can work out a resolution together. Do this a few times and your people will want to solve problems. They'll also understand that they don't have to run to you with every little thing. For a lot of people, that kind of responsibility is empowering. It allows them to grow into and expand their role in your business. They may not always have the perfect solution, and they could fail. Give them the freedom to fail, within limits.

WE'VE BEEN TRAINED TO EXPECT AN IMMEDIATE RESPONSE

I sort of blame Amazon for this, along with Uber Eats, Instacart, and all the other immediate service providers that have trained us to expect (demand?) instant results—like grabbing fast food versus packing your lunch. As of the writing of this book, you can purchase a vehicle online and pick it up from a local vending machine, thanks to Carvana. Those companies have large networks of people and infrastructures to manage the demand. You and I—especially you, as a new business owner—are each just one person, trying to do it all. We cannot deliver the clothes, the food, and the car at the drop of a hat. Though we may have people in our lives who expect that kind of service.

Business owners are constantly putting themselves in other people's shoes. We have to look at our business, product, services, advertising, and staff from our customers' points of view: "Is this a place I want to do business with?" We look at the day-to-day work and the work environment from our employees' points of view: "Is this the right job for me?" While you're developing those skills, don't expect everyone around you to do the same. We are all naturally self-centered, and working for someone else or becoming their customer lends a sense of entitlement. So don't be surprised by people who don't understand you are juggling a hundred other things when they bring you their problem. They are not seeing the world from your perspective, only theirs.

If someone is persistent, encourage them to schedule time with you. Calendaring apps allow you to send anyone a scheduling link, and you set your own "office hours" in the app. You might open up two hours, two days a week, for example, when employees can bring you issues that can't be handled with a simple text message.

LIMIT NOTIFICATIONS

Have you ever had lunch with someone whose phone constantly pings? They have notifications set up for voicemails, emails, text messages—even social media responses! It's nuts. Maybe they don't understand how cell phones work. Or they could have those notifications turned on intentionally to keep themselves busy and feel like they're accomplishing something. Consider all the forms of communication and how you would like to be notified for each one. You'll probably end up switching many of them from "sound" to "vibrate" and from "vibrate" to turning off notifications completely. This comes down to controlling incoming communication so it doesn't control you.

In the beginning, you're reacting to issues. You'll soon find the same issues repeating themselves. Figure out a solution and document it. This gives you a process for handling the same problem every time without starting from scratch. If you can hand the process off to an employee, delegate it properly. Train the person on how to implement the process and encourage them to improve it.

PROTECT YOUR DEEP WORK TIME

If your business is set up like a traditional office, limiting communication by phone, email, and text isn't enough. People will walk into your office. You may have to institute a physical sign for when you need quiet time to work on the business. This can be as simple as a "do not disturb" sign on your door. If you have cubicles or an open plan, designate some kind of sign and make it visible, like a hazard sign, a stop sign, or a flag. This signals to others that you are not to be disturbed. Encourage your employees to do the same if it makes sense for their role.

CALENDARING TO MANAGE STRESS

Surprises, both good and bad, are stressful. Blocking out time on your calendar for meetings, specific projects and activities, and tasks limits the surprises. You can see what you have planned, and you'll be more apt to stick to the plan. Likewise, other people see when they have time scheduled with you, and they'll be less likely to pop in uninvited and unexpected. Schedule the work and activities that allow you to decompress. Be intentional about the times of day when you schedule the most difficult work. If you start to slow down around three o'clock, that may not be the best time to schedule your toughest work. It may be the perfect time to go to the gym. The physical activity will wake you up and give you energy to finish out the rest of the day. If you know your stomach's going to be grumbling around noon, it doesn't make sense to start a hard project at eleven, because you will be thinking about how hungry you are the whole time. That may be a better time to tackle email.

If you have a particularly stressful event coming up, schedule something easy after. That might be a great time to go for a walk, for example. Knowing you have that walk coming up will make the stressful activity less daunting because you have something to look forward to after it's done.

PRIORITIZE YOUR BUSINESS NONNEGOTIABLES

Prioritizing your business nonnegotiables will help avert stressful situations. Next to making sure my people get paid, my top priority is keeping my people safe. This means safe working conditions in the office, on the road, and on-site at customer locations.

I probably spend more time than many business owners on safety protocols. Knowing we have them in place lowers my stress level. This includes things like two-way cameras in the fleet vehicles facing the driver and the road, through the windshield. This gives me visibility into my drivers' activities on the road. I can see whether they're wearing their seat belts and make sure they aren't taking on passengers or driving while impaired (although this happened once, and now I have an instant viral video if I were to ever post it). The outfacing camera records their progress and what's going on in traffic in case there's an accident.

After safety and payroll, everything else is secondary. Bad reviews, even lawsuits—you can deal with all of it, but hurting your staff is hard, if not impossible, to come back from. Fortunately, you can prevent these problems by having systems in place, and understanding why you have to spend time on those important/not urgent matters.

IMAGINE THE WORST-CASE SCENARIO

In his book *The 4-Hour Workweek*, Tim Ferriss recommends asking yourself, "What's the worst that could happen?"[42] This sounds counterintuitive. Won't imagining the worst outcome cause more stress? Not exactly. Say a customer threatens to leave you a bunch of one-star reviews and blast you online. If they actually follow through, will that physically harm you, your family, or your employees? Will it cause you to miss payroll? Will it put you out of business? It's safe to say that the answer to all those questions is no. The customer's a hothead—you know this from interactions with him. He exaggerates every problem and is never satisfied, no matter how hard you try to please him. Will other people take him seriously? That's hard to say. So let's imagine the worst: he does what he says he's going to do. Most of your customers and prospective customers probably won't see those reviews. You have so many great reviews that a few one-star ratings aren't going to bring down the average that much. Some sites will recognize they're coming from the same guy and delete them. As for the ones that remain, some people will believe them and others will not. How much is that really going to hurt your business? It might cost you a few customers, but so will a million other things. Weather events cost customers. Political events cost customers. Economic downturns cost customers. COVID cost a lot of businesses a whole lot of customers. Surely we can survive a few one-star reviews. When you look at it that way, the stress dissipates. Even the worst-case scenario isn't that bad. It's not knowing that's bad. Not knowing is like the monster under your bed. So look under the bed. Imagine the worst. Now you know, and now you can relax.

> Even the worst-case scenario isn't that bad. It's not knowing that's bad.

---

42 Timothy Ferriss, *The 4-Hour Workweek: Escape 9–5, Live Anywhere, and Join the New Rich* (Harmony, 2009).

DON'T LET WORK STRESS AFFECT
OTHER AREAS OF YOUR LIFE

The effects of stress at work can impact your life at home. If you're eating dinner and thinking about a customer complaint, you'll miss a great meal and the company of your family. It's easy to get sucked into a constant stress cycle, dealing with one problem after another, allowing the stress to build, and then taking it home with you. Often those problems don't deserve the attention we give them. If it's not something that's going to impact your life in five years, maybe it doesn't deserve another five minutes of your time.

Constant worrying is a hard habit to break, but we can do it. Just because we allowed ourselves to react to situations a certain way doesn't mean we can't retrain ourselves to have different responses. If we take a step back and view our reactions as an outsider, we see how much they hurt us rather than help us. As business owners, we have to help ourselves. No one else is going to step in and do it for us.

Understanding how your stress will increase and what you can do about it allows you to take on greater and greater challenges without the ill effects stress causes. Stress motivates us to perform at a high level when without it, we wouldn't.

PERIODIC CHECK-INS ON YOUR STRESS

Make a habit of evaluating your stress level. Does your stress match your actual situation? In the big scheme of things, is whatever you're feeling stressed about really that important? Is it going to be a problem tomorrow? Will you even remember it next week? Stress is part of our makeup, but it's a survival mechanism designed to help us survive. If our life's at risk, that stress kicking in to get our attention and drive us to action is a good thing. But having that same reaction over a bad review or a bank that can't do a simple transaction isn't practical or healthy. Again, it comes back to controlling what you can and letting the rest go.

Stress can hit you all at once, like when there's a catastrophic event—say your building burns down. But more often, stress creeps up on you. You don't even know it's happening—you only know that you're not happy and you don't feel well. It's harder to concentrate, and you might even feel like giving up and going back to your old job.

This is why you have to be intentional about managing stress. Use proactive routines to get ahead of it and relieve it. I get up before everyone else in my house and spend some time going over my plans and goals for the day. I have time scheduled for breath work and meditation during the day. These exercises take only a few minutes, but they act as a mental and emotional reset, wiping out the stress that's built up and preparing me for the next challenge.

You might think I have an inordinate number of challenges, but I don't have any more than the next person. If you're a business owner, you know what I'm talking about. If you haven't launched your business yet, you'll find out soon enough. Stuff happens that you do not expect. For example, I've been trying to pay a bill from my own business account for the past week. My bank keeps rejecting the payment, treating the transaction as fraud. I'm not kidding. It's my money and my bill. I've called them. I've emailed them. They can't seem to sort it out. If you're old enough to remember what a nightmare it used to be calling the cable company or the phone company when crazy charges showed up on your bill, and you got transferred to five different people before one of them accidentally disconnected you, it's kind of like that. There's not much you can do about it, and it's enough to drive you mad.

In *The 7 Habits of Highly Effective People*, Stephen Covey distinguishes between an individual's circle of influence and their circle of concern.[43] A person's circle of influence is much smaller than their circle of concern. Yet we still try to control it, and when we can't, we get frustrated. The key is to focus on what you can control (circle of influence) and accept the rest. Fighting what you cannot control won't help. Worrying about it won't help. Doing those things takes

---

43   Covey, *7 Habits*.

away from the time you could be working on those things within your control.

When I get irritated with the bank, I remind myself that the only way I can control the problem is to switch banks, which is definitely an option. But switching banks isn't as easy as changing your shoes. Do I want to take on the stress of shopping for a new bank, switching over my accounts, and so forth, or accept the fact that my bank struggles to make payments from my account and hope that someday they figure it out? Whichever I choose, I can't let it get to me. There is too much within my control that warrants my attention, and my business will do better—and I'll move closer to freedom—by focusing on those matters. But ultimately, it is my decision, and when I consider this, that I am choosing the lesser of two evils, it helps me destress.

MAKE DESTRESSING A DAILY ROUTINE

Morning routines are popular. How many of us have end-of-the-day routines? Letting go of the workday's stress before you go home to your family puts you in a better mood to enjoy their company. Instead of rushing home, take a few minutes to review your day and congratulate yourself on all that you've accomplished. Do some breath work. Meditate. Leave one hour earlier a few times a week and go to the gym. An end-of-day routine to help you wind down at home will improve your sleep too. Read something for fun—not work-related. Start a gratitude journal. If you can't think of anything to be grateful for, consider the fact that you're living in a first-world environment with running water and fresh air. You have a roof over your head and food to eat. Your family and staff are safe. Look around you and appreciate all that you have. People stress about what they don't have, but no one will ever have everything. So, should we allow ourselves to be in a constant state of stress over what we don't have? That's no way to live.

As part of my morning journaling, I write down three things I'm grateful for every day as part of my morning routine. Then I write down three things I'm excited for that day. If I have an extremely busy day planned, I pick something—like a meeting—that I may not be excited about, and I convince myself to look forward to it. Surprisingly, this trick works, and as the time approaches, I get excited about that meeting.

You can do this in the morning and at night to shift your mindset from "stressed out and negative" to "happy and relaxed."

FOR READERS ALREADY STRESSED OUT

Entrepreneurs don't always see stress as a serious problem. We're very good at taking care of the many moving pieces of our businesses, but we suck at taking care of ourselves. Sure, we might run, go to the gym, and do all those things that make us appear healthy on the outside, but we neglect what's going on inside. Before you start your business, put together a plan for managing stress. It's coming, and you can't avoid it completely. Whether you're getting ready to launch your business or already in the thick of it, put stress management on your to-do list and consistently address it. I've provided a few ideas for decreasing the stress inherent to business ownership and managing it when it happens. You can do what I do—set boundaries, calendar, meditate, do breath work, exercise, and journal—or come up with your own plan. Find something you can do and that you'll stick with. If you only squeeze in a ten-minute walk after work instead of driving to the gym, that's fine. Make your stress relievers realistic and do them consistently. As Tony Robbins has said, "How do you transform your state of mind, even when you're dealing with immense stress? The secret is in moving your body."[44]

Stress can affect your work in serious ways. It can turn you pessimistic and demotivate you. That's not a good place to be. It can cost you your business. When the stress gets to a point that you can't seem to turn it around on your own, you may need to seek professional

---

44 Tony Robbins, "How Do I Change My State of Mind?" *Inspirational Blog from a Professional Life Coach*, accessed December 14, 2024, https://www.tonyrobbins.com/blog/how-to-reset-your-mind-and-mood.

help. There's no shame in getting help for problems like stress. Again, as a business owner, you have to look out for yourself. There's no management in charge of your happiness and well-being. It's all on you. Take that responsibility seriously and seek help when you need it.

PACK YOUR LUNCH TO PROACTIVELY HEAD OFF STRESS

Your sacrifice is increased stress. It's unavoidable. But you can head it off to have less stress and manage it so it doesn't cause long-term damage.

Stress will come from a lot of different places, including some you never expected. Owning a business brings many people into your life that you wouldn't necessarily come into contact with in a regular job. Employees and customers are looking to you for help, guidance, service, and a paycheck. They'll bring you their problems, both work-related and personal. Their problems become your problems, adding to your stress load.

Stressful incidents sit in our minds and distract us from the important work that must be done. This doesn't mean we can ignore problems. If the cause of the stress needs to be resolved, we have to take care of it. But again, we have to look at our priorities. Stressful situations that are less important than the work at hand can be set aside and dealt with at another time. Otherwise, they are distractions, and we know what distractions can do. Business owners do not have the luxury of time or mental space to devote to minor issues when we have major responsibilities to manage. Learning to control our focus can go a long way toward eliminating stressful thoughts so we can accomplish what we set out to do.

In the short term, expect it and plan for it. Separate the good stress from the bad, and use the good stress to motivate yourself. Remember, your response to stress is everything. You can let it affect your emotions and your thinking, or you can put it in its place and focus on what's within your control. Over time, you will get better at dealing with stressful situations, especially as the same unavoidable issues come up again and again. You'll also solve problems along the way to reduce the avoidable ones.

Sociologist Chelsea Erieau has been quoted as saying, "Stress acts as an accelerator: it will push you either forward or backward, but you choose which direction."[45] By reframing stress as a small sacrifice that's necessary to become a business owner, and by harnessing good stress to motivate you toward your goals, you'll see the good in stress while managing the bad.

Recognize stress and its impact on your life and your business. Use it as a motivator and to increase rather than limit your productivity. You'll be able to work at higher levels of intensity for longer periods of time without burning out or suffering from the potential physical and emotional side effects of stress.

When I first became a business owner, I was confused about the stress I was feeling. I didn't understand what was going on, but I was able to get a handle on it and, over time, learn to manage and relieve it. If I had known then what I know now, I would have prioritized stress management as a critical piece of my business plan. Luckily, I discovered methods along the way and didn't have to suffer the long-term effects of prolonged stress. Now when I start a business, I go in with my eyes wide open, knowing my stress will increase. I'm more aware of the symptoms of stress and know the difference between eustress (good) and distress (bad). When everything doesn't go perfectly with my business, I take a deep breath, deal with what I can control, and move on from the rest. You will get there too. With every challenge, every problem, every unexpected turn of events, you'll manage and move on. And you won't let stress win. You will learn to employ stress to push you forward, not hold you back.

45   Richard Amaral, "Four Ways Stress Can Be Helpful," Psychology for Growth, February 10, 2024, https:// psychologyforgrowth.com/2024/02/10/four-ways-stress-can-be-helpful/.

PACK YOUR LUNCH QUESTIONS AND ACTIONS

1. Rate your *current* stress level on a scale from 1 to 10.
2. Rate your *average* stress level on a scale from 1 to 10.
3. What are the top three things that cause you stress?
4. What are your top three stress coping mechanisms?

9

YOU WILL HAVE TO BECOME OKAY WITH FEELING OUT OF CONTROL

"The goal isn't to get rid of all your negative thoughts and feelings; that's impossible. The goal is to change your response to them."

—AMIE DEAN

One day after church, a woman approached me to say hello. She and her husband had opened a rock climbing gym not far from my house. I had taken my daughter to a birthday party there a week earlier. I told her how much my daughter enjoyed the party and asked her how the business was going.

"Well," she said, "to tell you the truth, we're so stuck in the day-to-day operations that we can't come up for air. We'd love to find a manager to take over, but there doesn't seem to be anyone ready for the job."

I knew that feeling well. After all, I had handed the reins of many businesses to other people. It was always uncomfortable. They were never 100 percent ready. After putting so much effort into a business, the last thing I wanted to do was trust it to someone who wasn't as capable as I was—or worse, didn't care as much as I did.

I also knew that attitude would keep me from ever launching another business, and as far as freedom went, forget it. I offered the woman my advice: "No one is going to be ready until after they've been in the job awhile. Think back to when you started—were you ready? Whomever you hire will be in the same situation, except they'll have you to rely on until they get the job locked in. How great is that?"

She was surprised by my response and confided in me that she was hoping to find someone who could just walk in and take over. That kind of thinking isn't realistic. The best manager in the world couldn't just step in. Even someone who had managed a rock climbing gym of the same size in the same town couldn't take over without time to ramp up and learn the nuances of their climbing gym. The best you can hope for is someone honest and reliable with management experience who knows how to treat employees and customers. Everything else can be learned. And the management experience isn't even a requirement, because that can be learned too.

Finding the right person and taking that leap of faith is scary, though. Businesses are personal to business owners. They're like our children. We "birthed" them, raised them, and watched them grow. We don't want to trust them to just anybody. We want that perfect person to walk in and say, "Yes, I promise to love your children as much as you do, and I will do everything in my power to ensure them a bright future." If you've ever dropped off your kids at preschool, you know that's not going to happen. They're going to do the best they can with the resources they have, and that has to be good enough. And in a lot of cases it is.

Though that gym owner believed no new manager would be ready to take over, my thinking was "It's *you* that isn't ready. And not only will you not know if *they're* ready until after they start, but *you* certainly won't be ready either. You will never feel ready to replace yourself until *after* someone is already doing your job and proves themselves to you."

If entrepreneurs waited until they were 100 percent ready to start a business, there would be no new businesses. Again, it's like having kids. You have no idea what you're in for until it's too late. Sometimes ignorance is bliss.

The real problem for the woman with the gym—and the problem I had realized in myself when I hired managers—was the loss of control. How could I willingly give up control of my "baby" to someone I barely knew? Over time, letting go of control became a theme. Until I could trust other people to do their jobs, I would be overworked, which was bad for me. I'd also be the bottleneck at work, which was bad for my business.

You have no doubt heard the Serenity Prayer, popularized by twelve-step programs like Alcoholics Anonymous: "God grant me the serenity to accept the things I cannot change, the courage to change the things I can, and the wisdom to know the difference." There are some things that you cannot change, and so it is in your best interest to let go of control. You should even give up control of some things that you *can* change to focus on more important things.

Imagine having to make, or at least approve, every single decision. Operating that way is exhausting for you, and it slows down business. Of course, if you do not want to grow your business and you're okay with working "in the business" full time—versus on the business, taking care of those important/not urgent activities—that's fine. Just understand what you are giving up: a lot of your time and any hope of freedom for you and growth for your business. The benefit of this sacrifice is the opportunity to focus on growing your business. This is where you can effect the most change.

You will not always be in control. Giving up some control is the sacrifice you must make to protect yourself and grow your business.

DON'T BE AFRAID TO DELEGATE

You've no doubt heard of the Pareto principle, otherwise known as the 80/20 rule, which claims 80 percent of outcomes result from 20 percent of the causes. This is a general rule and not a hard-and-fast law of physics by any means. But it applies to many circumstances, especially in business.

Dan Martell, in his book *Buy Back Your Time*, notes that when it comes to work, "80% done by somebody else is 100% freaking awesome."[46] Or as I like to say, "80 percent done by somebody else is better than 100 percent done by you."

Delegating work just makes sense. After all, you hired people to do a job. You looked over their résumé, interviewed them, spoke with their references, and onboarded and trained them. You gave them all the tools they need to succeed. Given the chance, they'll probably do a better job than you, if not right away, then in time. They'll never improve if you don't give them a chance. Instead, you'll always be doing that job you hired them to do.

What if you don't hire people to do that 80 percent? Maybe you're afraid of letting go. If you spend your time on that 80 percent, who will do the 20 percent that only you can do? Your business suffers when you don't delegate. That unwillingness to be okay with not having control actually hurts your business instead of helping it. Along with your business, you're also hurting yourself. Spreading yourself too thin over too many tasks takes a toll, and you'll burn out.

Eighty percent done by somebody else is
better than 100 percent done by you.

---

46 Dan Martell, *Buy Back Your Time: Get Unstuck, Reclaim Your Freedom, and Build Your Empire* (Portfolio, 2023), 38.

It also harms your employees because maintaining constant control is micromanaging. When you micromanage people, they aren't allowed the opportunity to learn, make decisions, and grow. They don't feel as if they are part of the business, but instead just a hired hand doing someone else's bidding. That leads to a lack of fulfillment. If they really need the job, your people may stay around awhile in this environment, but they won't be happy. They may "quiet quit"—show up and do the bare minimum to stay employed. Or they may leave. Either way, they will never become the skilled and committed workforce you want them to be. They won't improve in their jobs, and they will never get to practice decision-making, management, leadership, and other skills necessary for them to become more valuable in their positions and perhaps be promoted at some point. That's the definition of a dead-end job.

It's tough to give up control when you know exactly how you want something done. In some careers, repeating a process to a T is critical. Brain surgery, for example. Maybe rocketry. But we have more leeway in most businesses. My preference is to hire good, capable people, give them the tools and training they need to do their jobs, and explain the outcome I'm looking for, then allow them to develop a way to do it. They can come to me for guidance and support, but I want them to use their own experience, insights, and creativity to do their jobs.

You provide the what and the why; they provide the how.

There *are* people who want to be micromanaged, usually for one of two reasons. The first is they just don't want to think that hard. They want someone else to figure everything out for them. It's easy and absolves them of any responsibility if things go wrong (e.g., "I'm only following orders").

The second-most-common reason is a lack of confidence. They may come from jobs where they were micromanaged and don't know anything different. It's up to you to encourage them to do their best, without fear of being punished if their solution isn't as good as what you expected. They can and probably will improve.

People who are unwilling or afraid to work independently under proper leadership will change, or they'll fail. People who are naturally autonomous will thrive. But try to micromanage them and they will not stay. Delegating work and giving people the tools and training to excel frees up your time and makes for a healthier, happier work culture. People are a reflection of your leadership, and you must give them space to breathe.

YOU CAN'T DO IT ALL FOREVER

When you start a business, you do it all. As soon as you can hire people, you have to hand off some of your work. Research shows that autonomy and a sense of ownership are essential for individual members to thrive and for your team to operate at its best.[47]

Delegating isn't only best for your employees, customers, and business, it's also critical for you. If you can't trust other people to do the work, you'll never get a day off. You'll never have a vacation. You'll never have any kind of freedom with your time (and isn't that one of the main reasons you started in the first place?).

You might think you'll never get into this situation, but I see it every day in my interactions with other business owners. They start companies thinking they're going to hire people and enjoy a life of leisure someday, but that day never comes. They are in their businesses every day. Couples who start businesses together make the same mistake. One of them is in the business at all times, and so they never get time together outside of the business. That's not a good recipe for a happy relationship.

In *Who Not How*, Dan Sullivan notes, "You can't have an innovative, increasingly more profitable company until it's a self-managing company with the day-to-day activities of running the business managed by your team."[48] Until you have people in the weeds taking care of the details, you can't be up in the helicopter looking over the entire

---

47 Sullivan and Hardy, *10x*, 89.

48 Dan Sullivan and Benjamin Hardy, *Who Not How* (Hay House, 2020), 206.

forest. From up there, you'll get a better view and envision your business five and ten years down the road. You'll imagine new products and services and see how your business can change to leverage new technologies and how it needs to change to remain competitive as the industry evolves. You'll look ahead at potential synergies to develop with partners. You'll look at your financial needs, too, and think ahead about the capital you need to raise in the coming years and how you'll do that. Sullivan, in *10x Is Easier than 2x*, further notes, "your team relies on you enabling them to be self-managing so that you, as the entrepreneur and visionary, can spend most of your time in your 20 percent genius zone."[49]

The stages of an entrepreneur are first, they do what they *have* to do, then they do what they're *good at*, and finally, they do what they *want* to do. You can't skip any stages. You have to start at the first one and work your way to stage three.

I've known entrepreneurs, often technically skilled people, who only want to do what they're good at—say, baking muffins. So they skip the "have to do" stage and spend their days baking muffins. You can imagine how that works out. Someone has to order the flour, buy the ovens, and pay the rent on the bakery. Someone has to hire baker's helpers so they're not working twelve hours a day, seven days a week. Somebody has to do payroll. Other entrepreneurs don't even want to do what they're good at—they want to jump right to stage three, doing what they want to do. So they might spend a lot of time posting ads for their bakery on social media. Meanwhile, no one is baking the muffins, and people are showing up hungry.

If the helicopter analogy doesn't work for you, think of your business as a boat. You need to be at the helm, steering the ship and deciding where to go next. You can't see what's ahead if you're down below or focused on rowing. If your head's down and you're focused on what's going on below, you won't recognize the dangers ahead. You won't see the competition or changes in the industry, the market, and

---

49   Sullivan and Hardy, *10x*, 89.

technologies. As you move through the stages, you have to give up some control over what you were doing to other people so you can move on to the next stage.

IT'S GOOD FOR YOU, YOUR BUSINESS, AND YOUR PEOPLE

Giving up control to people who aren't as invested in your business as you are is tough. Accept that they will likely never care as much as you do, but they can care enough to do a great job. You can encourage people to take ownership—and take pride—in the work if you give them work to do that helps them improve their skills and perhaps fulfill their own personal dreams in the future.

This shift in mentality—away from your needs and your business's needs in favor of those of your employees—isn't always easy, especially for people who have been in business for only a few years. Our conversations with staff revolve around the business and what we can do better to improve it. Putting that aside to consider what we can do to make our staff's lives better in and beyond the business doesn't come naturally. This is why you have to be intentional about it with initiatives such as quarterly evaluations. These one-on-one meetings are useful for discussing each employee's standing, but you can also include conversations about their future plans and what you can do to help them achieve those plans. Ask them where they see themselves in the company in a year, three years, five years. Is there another position they would like to pursue, and what kind of training would that require? Is this something you can provide in-house, online, or through a mentoring or shadowing program with you and other employees? Help them set professional goals and see which ones would be more achievable with your assistance. You don't have to agree to everything, but if you don't ask, they may never tell you. They may have experience or interest in a skill they are not applying in their current job and that they would like to develop further, perhaps as a way to improve their performance in their current role or a different one.

It takes time to develop an employee's trust. Often they initially tell you what they think you want to hear. They aren't going to tell you they're unhappy with a job they really need. Have regular conversations with them. Listen and learn about them—who they are as people, not just what they have to offer you. Over time, they will come to trust you, and then you can have honest discussions about their professional future.

Bringing people on comes with growing pains. It takes time to train people. Train—not micromanage. Training can be ongoing as new technologies, services, products, processes, and goals are introduced. Your people will come to you for guidance. This is time you have to put into the business by training them yourself or hiring someone else to do it. But you aren't responsible for training everyone, just the people "directly below" you. I'll spend time training a CEO of one of my businesses so he can then train the upper management, and so forth.

Another growing pain that appears as you hire people is that your customers may not want to work with anyone but you. This is a common issue that you can expect, but don't give in to the pressure. Use your time wisely and allow your people to do the work they were hired to do. Your customers will get used to it. They have to because you can't do that other job forever—you have a company to run.

LETTING GO OF CONTROL WITH OTHER PEOPLE

Your level of passion for your business will not be shared by others—not your employees, and not anyone else either. And you can't make them care. Looking back, I probably bored people to death with conversations about my business. You know when someone has a hobby or sport that consumes them, and that's all they talk about? That was me with my business (still is). That will be you too. Get excited, but don't expect anyone else to feel the same way. And don't hate them for it. They have their own passions, and if you stop talking about your business for one minute, they'll tell you about them. It took me a while to learn that lesson!

You might think all your relatives, friends, and neighbors will want to be your customers. This is something else you can't control. I've had friends hire other companies because they were cheaper. No matter how much I wanted to tell them why they were cheaper, and why they were probably going to regret their choice, I learned to keep my mouth shut and let people make their own decisions. When it's your business, it's so hard to do this because, again, we're talking about your baby. Your pride and joy. Why would anyone go with somebody else's baby? But you have to let it go.

LETTING GO OF CONTROL WITH EMPLOYEES

Amy was one of my earliest hires. She was a fantastic person and administrative assistant. Amy's desk was located in the front lobby, and my adjoining office had a window that looked out onto the area. One day I was grinding away, and it felt like I was barely keeping my head above water. There was so much to do. This was very early on, and I was putting in long hours every day. I glanced out my window into the lobby and saw that Amy was staring up at something. This was October in Michigan, so it was cold out. Amy had her coat and boots on. Her purse, which was usually tucked away in a drawer, was sitting on her desk, and she had both hands on it. I leaned over in my chair to get a look at whatever she had her eye on and realized it was the wall clock! The instant the second hand hit the twelve, signaling five o'clock, Amy was out of her chair, purse and gloves in hand. She waved goodbye and was out the door.

I had been so busy, I thought it was much earlier. The day had gotten away from me. But that's not what bothered me. What really irked me was how much of a hurry Amy was in to get out of there. Here I was, working my tail off to grow the company, and my assistant couldn't wait to get out the door. Why, I wondered, wasn't she knuckles-deep in work, oblivious to the hour—like I was? It didn't occur to me that she had a life outside of work and other priorities that had nothing to do with my business. I later learned that she lived with her mother and was her caretaker. So she was leaving work every day to go home to her second "job" of taking care of her elderly mother's needs. I had been so focused on my needs that I didn't think for a minute that the people I paid to support me had needs of their own.

Later, upon reflection, I was surprised by my response. I had taken her action so personally, like an insult to me and the company. I'm telling you this because it will happen to you. At some point you will realize that no one cares about your business as much as you do, and you have to be okay with that. It is not their job to care about your business as much as you do.

Just because your staff doesn't care as much about your business as you do doesn't mean they don't care. They do. They care about their job, and if you allow them to do it, they'll probably show you why they're better at it than you might be. If they aren't right away, it's possible they'll get there. You have to let them do it, and possibly fail, in order to achieve the kind of skill you expect. That takes time, and as a business owner, you do not have enough time to become an expert at every single facet of the job. As you bring on more people, you become more and more the big picture guy—the guy in the helicopter, the guy steering the boat, the boss.

People are not good at predicting what would motivate them to work harder. When asked, the typical answer is "money." Studies show that people are more likely to be motivated by working together to achieve a common goal. When you put your employees in that situation, you're likely to get their best work. They want to do good work naturally, and that desire is increased when they work with other employees to accomplish the company's goals. They do get a certain amount of fulfillment from that, and so you can help them and your business by creating an environment where that outcome is possible.

It's your job to help your vision become their vision.

Consider what happens if you micromanage people. Where does their fulfillment come from? Where does their motivation come from? It doesn't come from anywhere, because you snatched it away from them. Then you get to enjoy that stolen sense of accomplishment.

Hopefully, as a business owner, you don't need that kind of ego boost. You have enough going on already. Own the blame and pass on the praise.

Thomas J. Watson Sr. was the CEO of IBM. According to the story, a junior executive made a decision that resulted in a significant financial loss for the company, reportedly around $10 million. Expecting to be dismissed, the executive was instead met with understanding from Watson, who purportedly said, "Why would I fire you? I just invested millions in your education."[50]

I hope your employees never make a mistake that costs you millions of dollars, but they will make mistakes, and you have to let them. You have to let people fail so they can learn.

Instead of priding yourself on how good you are at every task, find satisfaction in the fact that you hired the right people and gave them the resources and the freedom to do their jobs. That makes you one smart, nonmicromanaging business owner!

DON'T BE A BOTTLENECK

A business owner I know was struggling to bring on new staff. He wasn't happy with a recent hire, so he instituted a new rule where he had to interview everyone before they were given an offer. With a very small business, this makes sense. But when you have a lot of businesses to run and people to manage, you don't have time to interview every candidate. As a result of his rule, new hirings were delayed and his current staff were being overworked. I advised him to

---

50 Nick Milton, "Jack Welch on Learning from Failure," *Knoco Stories* (blog), March 3, 2016, https://www.nickmilton.com/2016/03/jack-welch-on-learning-from-failure.html. While this story is widely circulated in business literature to illustrate the value of learning from mistakes, its authenticity remains unverified. Similar anecdotes have been told about other business leaders, but concrete evidence supporting these specific conversations is lacking.

pull himself out of the process because he was doing more harm than good to his people and the business. He had to be his own boss and make decisions that were best for the company instead of decisions that made him feel better.

This is easier said than done, but it's part of being a business owner. No one is going to tell you you're a bad business owner. You have to figure that out for yourself and then do something about it.

I'll say it again: *The stages of an entrepreneur are first, they do what they have to do, then they do what they're good at, and finally, they do what they want to do.* As you're figuring out which tasks to hand off to other people, use this as a mantra to guide your decisions and provide perspective. Keep your future goals in mind too: Where do you want to be in five years? Ten? What changes can you make right now to ensure that progression? Most importantly, how should you spend your time, and what can you hand off to someone else to get more time to devote to those things?

> The stages of an entrepreneur are first, they do what they have to do, then they do what they're good at, and finally, they do what they want to do.

WHICH TASKS SHOULD YOU DELEGATE?

At first, you'll be doing most or all of the work yourself. As soon as you can hire people, take a hard look at who will help your business move forward the fastest. Do you need someone to bake cupcakes? Take the orders? Take care of advertising or do the books? There will be tasks you're just not good at and others you excel at that take too much time and could be done by someone for much less money than your own time is worth at this stage.[51] If there's a role you could give up that would move your business forward, but you can't seem to give it up, ask yourself why. You might have a good reason, like you just can't find the right person yet. But remember, the perfect person may not exist. Sometimes you have to go with "good enough for now" and trust the person will get better as time goes on.

You might be hanging on to a task that's personal to you, such as those that involve customer contact. I was like this with my social media. I knew how I wanted to "talk" to followers, and I didn't trust anyone to represent my voice. However, I wasn't very good at social media. I needed someone who could produce posts and respond to followers quickly while maintaining consistency with my brand. I found someone who could manage that piece well, and now I don't have to worry about it. But giving it up was tough! The more the work is a reflection of me and my business, the more personal it feels. But I couldn't run multiple companies and do all the marketing, advertising, social media, and customer outreach. What got me to change my mind was looking at other companies' social media pages. They were doing it a lot better than I was, so I knew immediately that I needed to let go of my fears and hire a pro.

RELEASE CONTROL AND WELCOME FREEDOM

Giving up control is difficult, but it's a small sacrifice that pays off with a greater outcome. Letting other people in prevents you from being a bottleneck while leveraging the time and talents of other people, allowing you to scale your business. This gives you more time to spend on the business, from doing what you have to do, to doing what you're good at, to doing what you really want to do. Eventually, giving up control provides the freedom you desired in the first place, which is likely a main reason you started the business.

If you are willing to make the sacrifice of total control, your busi-

---

51   Martell, *Buy Back Your Time.*

ness will grow more quickly. You'll have more time to design and implement the long-term vision you see for your business, which no one else can do. Your business will thrive, and so will you, with time for your nonnegotiables too, like family and health. Your people will grow too, and you'll be building a team that trusts you and that you can trust—people you can trust your business with so you can take a day, a week, or a whole month off and know your company is in good hands.

Remember the woman with the climbing gym? She and her husband couldn't find the perfect hire to manage the place. They were overworked and frustrated, wondering if they'd ever get any time off. Well, they eventually took my advice and hired someone who wasn't 100 percent ready to step into their shoes but whom they had confidence in to learn the role on the job. This new person worked out so well that the couple was able to fulfill their dream of moving back to their home state of Idaho. As it turned out, they had grandchildren there and were missing out on the youngsters' lives. Hanging on to control of the gym had been limiting their lives, and once they got comfortable with having less control, they could fulfill a more important goal. That's the beauty of how a small sacrifice can change your life.

PACK YOUR LUNCH QUESTIONS AND ACTIONS

1. What are you holding on to that you should let go of?
2. List three tasks that you have to do, three tasks that you are good at, and three tasks that you want to do.
3. At this stage, what tasks do you need to do to add the most value to your business?

10

YOU WILL HAVE TO BECOME OKAY WITH FEELING ALONE

"The price of being a wolf is loneliness. The price of being a sheep is boredom."

—HUGH MACLEOD

Starting a business came with a lot of challenges. I expected many of them, but some issues caught me off guard. One thing in particular really surprised me.

No one ever asked me, "Allan, are you worried about how alone you're going to feel?" If they had, I would have laughed. *Alone? Me? Never. I'll have partners, employees, and customers. I'll probably go out of my way to be alone.* All that was true—over time, there were plenty of people involved. I had fifty-fifty partnerships in some of my companies, while in others I was a majority or minority owner. I still am. So feeling alone never entered my mind.

Until it did. Because it happened. I'd be working away, with people in the office and out in the field, and still feel completely alone. Part of the feeling was around no one caring about the business as much as I did. Part of it was the level of problems that were simply passed on to me. And yet another was just the nature of the beast.

This was even true of the businesses where a partner had an equal stake. I never felt as if they were sacrificing as much as I was, and that made me feel alone. I realize now how self-centered that perspective is. Of course they had made sacrifices. They were just different from mine, and so I didn't value them as much. But to the partners, they were just as important as my sacrifices.

My aloneness was intermingled with a feeling of imposter syndrome, feeling like I was operating out of my league and with no one by my side and no safety net.

Whenever I made a mistake or suffered a failure in my business, the feelings of loneliness were deep and painful. It was like a death spiral of emotions pulling me down, with no one to pull me out. Feeling alone is a weird conundrum when you're surrounded by employees and business partners. That aloneness, especially when it's brought on by rejection or failure, can spur feelings of imposter syndrome, where you question whether you're qualified to run a company. More than once, I've felt like it was me against the world.

When I began coaching other entrepreneurs, I found these feelings were not uncommon. My clients expressed similar feelings. In some cases, there was a partnership where one individual managed a part of the business, such as operations and hiring, and the partner managed another part, like marketing and outreach. When something went wrong within a person's domain, they felt alone. When their partner failed, they didn't experience that same aloneness. The reaction was more high energy, and sometimes anger, initially, followed by a drive to solve the problem. Perhaps the loneliness stems from failing at one's responsibilities, whereas when a partner fails, it's not so personal, and so the feelings are different. For solopreneurs, the aloneness occurs more often because they are responsible for everything. Like mine, those feelings of aloneness are often intermingled with a feeling of imposter syndrome.

The feeling of being alone is especially acute when you're rejected. Maybe a customer decides not to do business with you, a vendor doesn't want to work with you, or a key employee quits. They are saying no to your business, but it feels as if they are saying no to you—like they're breaking up with you. They may not see it that way at all, but for the person on the receiving end, that's how it feels.

Feelings of aloneness are often intermingled with a feeling of imposter syndrome.

One of the top complaints business partners have is that they do more than their partner. If the majority of partners think the other partner isn't pulling their weight, then obviously this is not the case. It's their perception. One reason for this is the amount of work required to start a business. If you're only doing half, and it's much more than you expected, you'll naturally assume the partner is doing much less. Don't be surprised if you're working away and, at the same time, imagining that your partner's off playing golf. The reality is they're probably as busy as you are.

Some of these feelings have to do with control, which we discussed in the last chapter. You'll feel like your partner doesn't care as much about the business as you do. They probably do, but you have no way of knowing that. And if they don't, there's nothing you can do about it. You can't make a person care.

I'm particularly sensitive to this in part because I value loyalty, likely to an unhealthy degree. When a business partner decided to quit the business, I took his decision personally. I felt betrayed. I tried very hard not to feel that way, but sometimes it's not possible to control how you feel. You can control your responses, but emotions just happen. It wasn't until another partner came to me and said that he was distancing himself from the partner that quit that I began feeling okay with the situation. It was the opposite of feeling alone: instead I felt seen, heard, and validated. I felt true loyalty.

I knew my reaction wasn't logical. No one should have to cut ties with another person just because they ended a partnership with someone else. Yet there it was. These are the kinds of feelings I did not expect at all. After a few days, I told the second partner I was okay with him reengaging with the guy who quit. I didn't want revenge. I wanted someone to know what I was going through, and the second partner showed me that. He showed me empathy, which is something all humans want, especially when we're going through difficult times.

While these emotions seem illogical at first glance, perhaps they should be expected. Entrepreneurs are very much on their own compared to employees working within a company. This might be one reason most people don't make a go of it and why so many who do fail.

During COVID, a lot of jobs moved from the traditional to the home office. I know people who thrived in the remote environment, but I know others who couldn't handle the isolation. One woman who worked in customer support said that having no one to commiserate with over difficult calls made the work unbearable. In an office, when you're having a tough day, you can chat with the guy in the next cubicle, and chances are he's been where you are and can empathize. But working remotely removes that ability—much like being a business owner separates you from your peers, leaving you to deal with tough times on your own.

The good news is that being alone is usually temporary because people will show up for you. You'll have proof that there are people in your life who understand what you're going through and want to support you. Knowing this enables you to manage these situations in the future. You may still have fleeting feelings of being alone, but just knowing other people can empathize makes those feelings easier to bear.

STRUGGLING WITH ALONENESS

I was training one of my earliest employees to become a manager. One day he called to tell me how badly his day was going. After listening for a few minutes, I offered my sympathy and support. Then I concluded by saying that my day was going much worse. I told him so and listed all the reasons. He didn't respond. Not a single "I'm sorry." No "Wow, your day sounds awful." Nothing. I was surprised, but I shouldn't have been. Complaints go up in a business, not down. You can listen to your employees' problems and offer support and advice, but you can't bring them all your problems. That's poor leadership. In my defense, this was very early in my career as a business owner, and I'm not proud of it. No one wants to be one-upped when they're having a bad day. Especially by their manager. Sheesh. He needed me to listen, not compare his problems with mine and essentially discount them.

Going to your employees with your problems is like asking your kids for financial advice. They'll probably look at you with their mouths open, thinking you've lost your mind. I imagine that's what the manager was doing on the other end of the phone. When you vent to people who depend on you or ask them how to fix a problem that you should be able to handle, they immediately start thinking about how it affects them. Imagine being an employee whose boss complains about financial problems the day before payday. What's the first question that pops into your head?

Employees will never be as attached to your business as you are. When you're in a partnership, each partner's responsibility to the company depends on their investment. The higher the investment, the greater the responsibility, particularly when it comes to finances. They share the upside and the downside, so if the company's doing well, they do well.

One of my business partners wanted more equity in our company, which had a substantial line of credit, in the neighborhood of $700,000. I explained to him that if he wanted 10 percent more of the company, he would be responsible for 10 percent more of the debt—$70,000. Partners don't always understand that the more equity they own, the more tightly bound they are to the business, the good, the bad, and the ugly. Frequently, employees don't even see the financial side of what we do, so they don't have that responsibility hanging over their heads. This is another reason they can come and go as they please. As business owners, it's not that easy.

Feeling alone is a necessary sacrifice of owning a business, and it's even lonelier when you don't have a business partner—like being a single parent where all the responsibilities fall on your shoulders and there's no one to commiserate with or ask for help. No one knows what you are going through, and so you internalize the problems and the stress. The aloneness increases as you grow your business, so you have to decide how much you can handle. You might decide to keep your business smaller for that reason.

When people leave your business, you feel like they're quitting you. I've felt rejected when people quit under the best circumstances, which confuses me because I want people to do what's best for them and their families. The feelings are worse when a partner or a high-level manager quits. These are the people you're closest to and whom you spend the most time with, and those feelings can linger for a long time. This isn't about refilling the position. It's about the person divorcing themselves from your business.

No matter how much you rationalize the decision, the emotions can still be overwhelming. I haven't felt this way over every employee who chose to leave. Some employees were difficult, and I wasn't sad to see them go. But the more understanding and kind they were, giving ample notice and leaving their work in good shape for the next person, the worse it felt. This might have something to do with realizing what a great person I'm losing versus the person who just stops showing up.

Ending a business partnership is very difficult, in part due to the disentangling involved. If an operating agreement is like a prenuptial agreement, dissolving a partnership is like a divorce.

When people leave, you question yourself and your business, even more so than if a customer is unhappy with your services or when a marketing plan doesn't deliver results. You know the person and consider them a colleague and, often, a friend. You think they're as invested in the business as you are, so when they leave, you feel betrayed. The reality is that they were working for a paycheck, and no matter how much they liked the company, they will always be looking for a better situation and more money. And sometimes they have life events that influence their decisions. You can improve their work environment, role, and salary—and you should consider those options throughout the person's employment—but many things are outside of your control.

People can leave because of you or the job. More often, it has nothing to do with you. Remember, your business is your dream, not theirs. You can create an environment and situation that promotes employee engagement, but at the end of the day, they will never feel the same way that you do about your business. Accept it, make your workplace a great place, and know that people will leave.

Some of the best businesses see people leave because they have prepared them for better roles in other companies or for starting their own business. This is when you really have to put your feelings aside and cheer that person on. They are bettering their lives, and you helped them do that. That's worth celebrating. Those relationships are still valuable, and you may be able to help one another out down the road. They could refer employees or customers to you, or you could enter into some type of partnership. They could become a customer and vice versa. Put the person ahead of the role they play in your business and what you get out of them, and you will win every time.

Suffice it to say, I don't follow Mr. Wonderful's thought process of "you're dead to me."

That mentality aligns with my nonnegotiable values. Consider the alternative: holding people back from realizing their dreams. Making people dependent on you so they can never do anything on their own is not good leadership and does not promote a healthy work environment. Instead, provide them with the training, tools, and opportunities to improve. Encourage their confidence in themselves. They may still leave, but they may also become so happy with the situation that they never want to leave.

World-class athletes and business leaders often suffer from depression after they leave their sport or company. Their identities are defined by their work, and when that work stops, they lose their sense of purpose. Similarly, seemingly healthy people who work for decades and then retire don't always live as long as they expect. Without something to strive for or an image to live up to, aloneness sets in, depriving them of joy.

In the Olympics, you'd think a gold medal winner would be the happiest, followed by the silver winner, and then the bronze medalist. Surprisingly, that's not the case. Bronze medal winners tend to be happier than athletes who take home silver. They're happy to have medaled and not come in fourth, whereas the silver medalists feel defeated because they didn't take home the gold.[52]

Take your business seriously, but don't let it define you. Don't let the company or its wins and losses consume you. Remember always that you are more than an entrepreneur, a boss, and a business owner. Develop other parts of your life, including those relationships and hobbies you sacrificed early on.

IT'S NOT ALL BAD

As people leave your business, you'll become more accepting of their choices and less affected by the feelings that follow. You'll hire new people and realize there's a lot of great talent out there. You'll gain confidence and resilience, and it will get easier.

Some entrepreneurs sacrifice the wrong things, and their loneliness is worse than it needs to be. For example, on Lex Fridman's podcast, Elon Musk described his mind as a "storm" and said, "I don't think most people would want to be me. They may think they'd want to be me, but they don't know; they don't understand."[53]

---

52 *The Weight of Gold*, directed by Brett Rapkin (Podium Pictures in association with Octagon, 2020).

53 Elon Musk, "Elon Musk: War, AI, Aliens, Politics, Physics, Video Games, and Humanity | Lex Fridman Podcast #400," interview by Lex Fridman, November 9, 2023, 2:12:50, YouTube, https://www.youtube.com/watch?v=JN3KPFbWCy8&ab_channel=LexFridman.

You don't have to choose that path. We each have our own nonnegotiables, but they should all include personal relationships outside of the business. You need that emotional support system to survive.

Being alone is more common today than it was in the past. How many of us spend hours in front of a computer screen, TV screen, tablet, and cell phone? When I was a kid, everyone in the family had an assigned seat at the dinner table, and we all showed up sans electronics. The food tastes better and the experience is better when you eat with other people. In fact, your body digests food differently when you eat with others, especially if you really like the people.[54]

Eating together is one way to build community, and that sense of community, or "tribe" as it's been called more recently, is critical to our health. In his book *The Blue Zones*, author Dan Buettner notes that longevity is not solely determined by genetics but is also influenced significantly by lifestyle, environment, and social factors, such as a sense of community. Buettner identified five regions in the world where people consistently live longer, healthier lives, and his research suggests that adopting specific habits and cultural practices can increase lifespan and improve overall well-being.[55]

One way to ease feelings of loneliness is to identify the causes and do something about them. You can't talk to your employees about all your problems, but you should be able to talk to your business partner and spouse, for example. And if you feel like you're working more than your partner, see if that belief is warranted. There may be a miscommunication between the two of you, and they work more than you realize. Or maybe you never sat down and outlined one another's responsibilities to the business, so they're under the impression that they're doing more than they should, while you're feeling shortchanged. Partnership relationships vary from silent to

---

54   Mary Beth Albright, "How Eating with Others Nourishes Us in More Ways than One," *The Washington Post*, February 26, 2023, https://www.washingtonpost.com/food/2023/02/24/food-health-well-being/.

55   Dan Buettner, *The Blue Zones: Lessons for Living Longer from the People Who've Lived the Longest* (National Geographic, 2009).

very active, and the relationship and associated responsibilities should be clear among all parties.

An operating agreement that includes the responsibilities of each partner can head off these misunderstandings and avoid the ensuing feelings of bitterness and aloneness. By establishing each partner's role up front and with clarity, you have a document to refer to whenever there's a question about each person's duties. This isn't a document to be used in a contentious way. The fact is that partners are likely to forget what they agreed to do early in the arrangement, which is why the document is important. Then you can revisit it to ensure each of you is holding up your end of the bargain, and you might also decide to revise it down the road. Prepare the agreement before the business launches officially. You and your partners may feel like this is an awkward first step, as if you're in adversarial positions. Agreeing on the details can take months or years, so if you come to an impasse, consider bringing in a third party to negotiate the operating agreement.

ENJOY THE JOURNEY, PASS ON THE LESSONS, AND VALUE THE CONNECTIONS

When I was a teenager growing up in rural Oregon, I had a sister at Cal State, in the Bay Area. My parents couldn't afford flights for the whole family, so we'd drive ten hours to visit sis. My brother and I always complained about the long trip, and Mom would remind us to enjoy the journey. Moms always say things like that, and teenage boys always ignore them. To save money on motel rooms, we'd sleep on the floor of my sister's tiny apartment. Suffice it to say that we did not look forward to those trips.

On one such drive, we weren't more than twenty minutes into our ten-hour trip when Mom suddenly pulled the van over, opened the sliding side door, and said, "Everybody out. We're going to enjoy the journey." We got out, thinking it was some kind of joke. Mom had parked the van in the gravel overlooking an expansive onion field. We were so confused. We had probably driven past that onion field hundreds of times, yet my brother and I didn't know it existed. And it was beautiful. I think that's when I finally understood the whole "enjoy the journey" thing. You have to pay attention to those moments of joy and beauty or they will pass you by. Now every time I drive by that onion field, I'm reminded of that lesson.

One of the main values a coach provides is the legacy they leave behind, played out through the careers of the players they coach and the other coaches they mentor. Hall of Fame BYU football coach LaVell Edwards has an impressive coaching tree that includes Division I college and Super Bowl–winning coaches, like the Kansas City Chiefs' Andy Reid. The coaching tree goes on forever, as each person impacted by that coach goes on to affect the lives of the people they coach.

Think of yourself as the head coach, mentoring people to be better at whatever career goals they wish to pursue within your business. When you think about it that way, you see how even when people leave your business, they're taking a part of you and what they learned under your leadership with them. Be proud of that and let those feelings of abandonment go.

If you have children, like I do, you know they're going to leave home someday. You love those kids, but sometimes—if they're like mine—they try your last nerve. If you didn't love them so much, their ups and downs wouldn't affect you so deeply. It's because you care that they get to you! It's like that with employees too. You may not love them like you do your children, but you care about them and you want them to do well. However, you have no control over their career decisions, so you have to live your emotions somewhere in the middle between caring and letting go. You might hire the best person for the job, invest in their training, and see them blossom into a rock star—then have to say goodbye because they found a better job somewhere else.

It's easy to get caught up in thoughts about how much you give your business partners and staff versus what you get back. A scarcity mentality can make you bitter. An abundance mentality, where you accept that there is plenty of great talent out there and you will find another rock star, can ease that bitterness and allow you to be happy for other people's successes, even when it takes away from your business.

A good relief from aloneness is talking to someone who understands what you're going through or someone who cares about you enough to be sympathetic. I've been lucky to have a very sympathetic spouse. She cares enough about me and what I want in life to sympathize when I'm going through a tough time.

Some business owners aren't so lucky. I've worked with business partners whose spouses are constantly pressuring them to work fewer hours, take a higher salary, or quit the business. It seems those spouses don't understand what it means to run a business and how personal it is to the business owner. If they did, and they truly cared about the person, they would be more supportive. Their behavior isolates their spouse, causing those feelings of being alone.

Professional networks are also a great place to talk to people about the ups and downs of being an entrepreneur. New business owners are afraid to talk to people in the industry because they see them as competitors, and they're afraid of giving away all their business secrets. That attitude won't serve you. Some of those people will be competitors, but you have more to gain by speaking with them than you have to lose by keeping your distance. You understand each other's struggles and can commiserate and help each other out. They might share tips with you about finding a good technician, and you can tell them where you've found the best sales staff. There are plenty of customers to go around.

You can meet people at trade shows and conferences and through masterminds. You can create your own industry-specific community, like I did. During COVID, as people lost touch with each other, I created a podcast called *Start and Grow Your Pest Control Company* and an associated community for pest control experts. In just a few years, and after a name change to Bug Bux, we've grown to be the largest pest control owner group on Facebook.

Don't shy away from people, thinking they'll steal your secrets. If I told someone everything I know about the bug business, the chances of them doing the work to implement every bit of advice are slim. There's a lot of work involved. Another thing to consider is that by sharing information, you are not only doing each other a favor; you're all becoming better equipped to serve your customers, so you're improving the industry as a whole. Everyone benefits from that.

If you join a group, participate in a productive way. Don't criticize others. Bring advice and be supportive. You can still discuss problems, but balance the negatives with positives.

Sometimes sharing a challenging situation can help other people feel like they're not alone. A while ago, I told my pest control community about an incident with a client. She wasn't a paying customer, but I had given her free service as part of our 501(c)(3) organization, Proof Gives Back. We made multiple visits to her home over two years to take care of a persistent problem. After the final service, she posted an online review—along with a one-star rating and a demand for her money back. We were all confused because her service was free. Exactly what money would we be refunding? It was a pro bono job through my nonprofit. After getting over the initial shock of the situation, I shook my head—and shared the story with my pest control colleagues. They got a huge kick out of it! No doubt they'd all had their share of strange customer experiences, and hearing my tale showed them not to take criticism personally, because there are strange customers everywhere.

Sharing stories also shows you how other people solve business problems and the outcomes. A colleague might try something that works well, and you can duplicate it. Or they might fail miserably, and if they're willing to share the experience in a judgment-free zone, everyone can learn from their mistake.

As you seek out people to talk with, be a good listener. Not long ago, I got a call from a friend. I thought he was calling me for business advice, but after listening to him talk for a while, I realized he didn't need me to say anything at all. He was just feeling alone and needed to talk to someone.

We're all very busy, and it's easy to end a call when the person on the other end doesn't explicitly need something from you. But we all need to take time to listen to each other. Be there for other people, and they'll be more likely to be there for you.

The isolation that solopreneurs, business owners, and people who work from home feel is real, and for many, it's unsettling. A conversation with someone willing to listen can go a long way toward helping a person get through the day. If they're in the same business as you, they can empathize, which is something you won't get anywhere else. Consider the fact that you could be that empathizer for the person who has no one else that understands their problems. Not their spouse, their partners, or their employees.

PACK YOUR LUNCH, BUT DON'T EAT ALONE

The aloneness you experience as a business owner seems illogical, but it's real, and it will surprise you. You'll suffer a rejection or a failure, become frustrated, and then—wham—a sudden feeling of aloneness hits you. No matter how many people work within your company, you'll feel as if you're the only one who cares. Though the feeling is actually very logical, the degree to which it affects you seems out of place. This is especially true for solopreneurs, since they have no business partners or staff to commiserate with over a business loss.

Aloneness is a sacrifice you have to make for the opportunity to run a business. The feelings may subside over time as you get accustomed to them and learn to manage them. Along the way, you'll learn whom to trust and depend on to get you through the toughest times.

Be aware of the many reasons people leave your business and understand that it's seldom intended as a personal affront to you. People have dreams outside of your business, and you can't hold them back to suit your needs. Learn to cheer them on. You may have contributed to their ability to improve their life in another position or another company, or even to start their own business. In that way, you've started your own "coaching tree."

Becoming resilient to loneliness, building a supportive personal and professional network, and understanding why people leave will help you deal with the aloneness of being a business owner. You'll build a strong support system over time and find your "ride or dies" that will be there when you need them, and you can be there for them too. Also, it is through this process that you learn a lot about yourself and how to respond to adversity.

PACK YOUR LUNCH QUESTIONS AND ACTIONS

1. Have you ever felt alone even though you were surrounded by people?
2. Do you struggle opening up to others and telling them about your emotions?
3. What are your top three tricks to overcome loneliness?

11

YOU WILL HAVE TO BE FLEXIBLE WITH YOUR IDENTITY

"You have to be willing to go to war with yourself and create a whole new identity."

—DAVID GOGGINS

I always thought of myself as very approachable in my leadership role. I had an open-door policy, and people who worked for me were comfortable coming to me with their concerns. Well, that's what I thought.

A couple of years into my first business, walking through the call center floor, I overheard a conversation about an unhappy customer. The customer was so unhappy that they threatened to leave bad reviews. I could tell the situation was serious. The kicker was that the problem had occurred days earlier and everyone knew about it but me. This was the sort of problem that I would want to know about right away. Why hadn't I been told?

I tracked down the customer service manager and asked her why she had kept the problem a secret. "I could have helped you," I said.

"You know you don't have to deal with these kinds of problems on your own."

I could tell she was struggling to respond, so I invited her into my office, where we had more privacy. Still, it took some prodding to get to the answer. I told her that she wasn't in trouble and her job wasn't at stake; I just had to know why I was the last person to hear about what was going on. Finally, she said, "Allan, you are really hard to talk to. You can be super scary, especially when there's a problem. I thought you'd yell at everybody."

I could not breathe. Her answer shocked me. Was I scary? Did I yell? And if I was so wrong about being approachable, what other false notions did I have about myself? All along, I had viewed my approachability as a true strength—something that separated me from all the bad bosses out there. I thought long and hard about my own behaviors and how they were out of line with what I was telling myself. I encouraged people to be autonomous, and I didn't micromanage them. However, when they acted autonomously and made a mistake, I was outwardly upset. That realization humbled me, and I am not easily humbled. I couldn't help but wonder what else I believed about myself that wasn't exactly true.

Thinking I was one kind of person and then realizing I was another was something I had to come to terms with, and so do you. It was the wake-up call I needed. In that moment, I realized I had to be open to the fact that other people saw me very differently from the way I viewed myself. That realization opened the door to real change. If I was to be the person I aspired to be, and actually thought I was, I had to get out of my head and view myself from a more objective perspective. The flexibility piece comes in when you accept that you may not be the person you thought you were and you accept the responsibility to change your behavior.

Thinking I was one kind of person and then realizing I was another was something I had to come to terms with, and so do you.

Flexibility with your identity doesn't require being flexible with your principles. Your values must remain. It's your strengths and weaknesses that you must become more aware of and honest about with yourself. That's not easy to do from inside your head, because we all have a pretty positive view of ourselves. Well, we should at least.

We have to be open to other people's opinions and sensitive to their responses to our behaviors. This comes down to emotional intelligence, which can be a lot to ask of someone who's also trying to run a business and manage a lot of people.

We wear many hats, and we are probably not good at wearing every one of them. We shouldn't fool ourselves into believing we're experts at everything, especially when it comes to interactions with other humans. If we do the books well or we do a good job at marketing, the outcome from these activities is obvious—we don't go broke, and we get more customers. But the outcomes caused by our behaviors toward other people are much more subtle. As business owners, we're in a position of authority, and our people aren't always going to tell us when we're doing something wrong. Instead, they become demotivated or quit. I'd prefer the criticism.

Be flexible with your identity. Allow yourself to experiment with who you are, without sacrificing the core elements of your identity created by a supreme being. Be open to changing the aspects of your professional entrepreneurial identity. You will uncover the very best of yourself.

DISCOVER YOUR STRENGTHS,
UNCOVER YOUR WEAKNESSES

Research shows that in a lot of cases the most successful people are the ones that try out multiple identities. Herminia Ibarra, a professor at London Business School, discovered that successful people don't just accept identities to please others. They figure out different roles to find what actually works for them.[56]

In his book *The Greatness Mindset*, Lewis Howes said, "to pursue greatness, you have to first know yourself. No one can do that for you. There are problems you are meant to solve. Don't miss out on knowing yourself and feeling completely fulfilled by the success meant for you."[57]

When I became aware of this phenomenon, I was focused on my shortcomings. However, being open to learning about your strengths and weaknesses goes both ways, and I also discovered strengths I didn't know I had. Consider people who go into business believing they aren't good at public speaking. Yet when called upon to speak in front of an audience, they sound as if they've been doing it their whole life. It's like a hidden talent they didn't know they had. Or maybe they struggled a bit, but with some training, they improved and became skilled speakers.

We all have preconceived ideas about ourselves, and not all of them are true. We might base these ideas on previous experiences, like maybe we tried something one time and didn't do well. That doesn't mean that we can't be good at it the second time or that we can't learn to be good at it. Other times, we believe we're incapable of something simply because we've never done it.

Be open to discovering your strengths as well as your weaknesses. Commit to working on your weaknesses and capitalizing on your strengths. This opportunity is especially available to business owners

---

56 Herminia Ibarra, *Working Identity: Unconventional Strategies for Reinventing Your Career* (Harvard Business School, 2003).

57 Lewis Howes, *The Greatness Mindset: Unlock the Power of Your Mind* (Hay House, 2023).

because we have so many different jobs within our companies. Over time, our weaknesses may become our strengths.

An employee is expected to be good at one thing or a few things. A business owner has to be good at many things. You don't have to be an expert at everything, but you need to know enough about everything your business does internally and what it provides to customers so you can have informed discussions with your colleagues, employees, and customers. You can't refuse to look at financial statements because you're not good at numbers, for example, or not read a contract because you're not a lawyer.

You may find strengths you didn't know you had. You'll also find weaknesses. This can make you uncomfortable, but don't shy away from the weaknesses. Be humble and embrace them. Humble is not the same thing as lacking confidence. In a lot of cases, it's the opposite. It's an attribute great leaders possess, especially when they leverage the knowledge of their weaknesses to adjust their behavior and commit to learning.

Commit to learn and do better. Be grateful for the opportunity to see your weaknesses and have a chance to improve. When you look at it that way, exposing your weaknesses is a gift.

BE HONEST WITH YOURSELF AND KNOW WHEN TO HIRE SOMEONE ELSE

Believing you are a certain type of person becomes a self-fulfilling prophecy. Children who are told they are stupid believe it, and they struggle to learn. Kids who are told they aren't athletic struggle at sports. They adopt what their parents tell them as their own internal dialogue and carry it with them into adulthood. It's the same with business owners who believe they're good or bad at something and repeat that dialogue in their heads. It becomes that self-fulfilling prophecy, and it does not always serve them.

The opposite of that negative dialogue are affirmations. These can be helpful, but we also have to be honest with ourselves. Telling ourselves we're good at something doesn't make it so. The affirmation could push us toward being better, but we still have to put in the work.

I'm a prime example of this phenomenon. I never saw myself as a "numbers guy." As a business owner, I had to become one. I purchased a college textbook on corporate finance, watched YouTube videos on the topic, and—lo and behold—discovered I was actually pretty good at working my way around financial statements and making business decisions based on what they were telling me.

Being a numbers guy didn't convince me to take on that role in my businesses, but it did allow me to have more-informed conversations with my CFOs and CPAs. As you scale your business, you'll have to hire people with more expertise in certain areas, but working on your weaknesses can help you make better decisions because you'll have a better understanding of what they are doing.

Your identity shifts depending on the role you fill. You might lean into a particular role and decide to hang on to it or decide to hire someone for the job. When I started my pest control business, I went to people's homes and sprayed for bugs. Then I hired other people to do it. But if we were short-staffed, I wouldn't allow the work to not be done. I'd jump in a truck and head to the customer site. Likewise, if there was a problem with billing, I'd never shy away from getting on the phone with a client to work it out.

As your company grows, think about the role you want to play in it. As I've said before, you start with doing what you have to do, then what you're good at, and then what you want to do. How quickly you move through those stages depends on you and your business. If you can't afford to hire for roles you don't want to do, you may have to do them longer.

PACKING YOUR LUNCH DOESN'T INCLUDE ONLY LEFTOVERS

When we start a business, we don't know what we'll have to do or learn. We don't know who we will have to become. You might start out packing your lunch with leftovers, but be willing to add more, depending on what your business needs. This means learning more and being more.

The roles aren't always clear-cut job descriptions. We might discover we need to be better leaders, better speakers, better listeners, or better communicators in general. We might realize, as I did, that we need to work on our social skills and be willing to step outside ourselves to see what other people see. Hard skills and soft skills come into play, and we can't predict all of our weaknesses. They become apparent when they're tested, and that gives us the opportunity to be humble, learn, and turn them into strengths.

We start businesses believing we're the masters of these inanimate things, but the truth is that our businesses are living, growing, evolving entities, and until they can grow without us, we are their servants. Adopt the attitude that you are a servant to your business until your business can grow without you. Be flexible and grow with your business. Otherwise, you'll be an obstacle. Being open to flexibility with your identity increases your likelihood of business success.

> Adopt the attitude that you are a servant to your business until your business can grow without you.

Your new roles may not be something you expected. They may be roles you don't believe you can take on or that you don't want to take on. A fellow business owner posted the question "In order to be a successful entrepreneur, do you believe you have to be good at sales?" I responded that you may not have to become your company's main salesperson, but you should have the soft skills of a great salesperson. You have to know how to motivate people. You have to be able to convince people to believe in your business, products, and services. This is a role new business owners may not be comfortable adopting, but they can learn. They can, and must, be flexible with their identity and do what's needed for the business.

No matter how well we plan, tasks will appear that we didn't prepare for. Being flexible with who we are and what we can do lets us fill whatever role our business requires in the short term as we sharpen our skills and decide whether to make the role permanent or hire someone to fill it.

PACK YOUR LUNCH QUESTIONS AND ACTIONS

1. What are the elements of who you are that are nonnegotiable?
2. Have you had an experience of turning your weaknesses into strengths?
3. Are there any skills that you would like to master that you're not currently good at but would be an asset for your business?

12

YOU WILL BECOME VULNERABLE

"A leader, first and foremost, is human. Only when we have the strength to show our vulnerability can we truly lead."

—SIMON SINEK

A few years ago Coinbase CEO Brian Armstrong made it known that his company supported the Black Lives Matter movement.

Until the movement adopted some messaging about defunding the police.

Armstrong did not follow that belief, and he didn't want his company connected to it either. But backing out of his support for the BLM movement was going to anger just as many people as staying in it would.

He made the brave decision to let his people know the company was changing direction and not supporting the movement, but he also took responsibility for backing it in the first place without fully understanding what it stood for. Then he offered a compensation package to anyone who wanted to leave the company due to this mixed messaging.[58]

Armstrong had put himself in a difficult spot, and he had to be vulnerable, admit his mistake, and make it up to his employees and other people who were affected. But his handling of the situation was critical to establishing the credibility and branding of his business.

The success of a business depends on the personal development of the owner. A business will never be able to achieve a level of success that is above that of its owner or leader. Issues within the business are often a reflection of the leader's shortcomings. A business owner might be able to hide their personal issues, but when their business has issues, they are immediately seen as the leader's flaws. When you create a business, you have to disclose a lot about yourself. You expose yourself to scrutiny. You may feel like you're under a microscope. You can use this situation to learn a lot about yourself and use other people's observations to improve. In this way, you can trade your weaknesses for strengths.

> A business will never be able to achieve a level of success that is above that of its owner or leader.

ALL YOUR FLAWS ON DISPLAY

You are especially vulnerable early on as the leader of a privately held company. For this reason, it makes sense to pack your lunch before

---

58 Tim Ferriss, "The Tim Ferriss Show Transcripts: Brian Armstrong, CEO of Coinbase—the Art of Relentless Focus, Preparing for Full-Contact Entrepreneurship, Critical Forks in the Path, Handling Haters, the Wisdom of Paul Graham, Epigenetic Reprogramming, and Much More (#627)," *The Blog of Author Tim Ferriss*, October 10, 2022, https://tim.blog/2022/10/10/brian-armstrong-transcript/.

entering the arena by mentally preparing yourself to receive criticism and scrutiny.

You will have to share a lot more information about yourself than you're used to sharing. Loans, tax applications, and disclosures require handing over personal financial records that take months to process. You will be asked to provide multiple personal financial statements, and you have to comply. These and other tasks make up the administrative vulnerability that you will face.

On the personal side, you open yourself up to scrutiny and often criticism. Through your advertising, services, and products, you expose who you are—by way of your business—to the world. Your employees see every mistake you make, and they also see how you handle those mistakes. So if you lose your temper or make a bad business decision, they'll notice. They may not say anything, but they see who you are. There are more eyes on you than ever, and that can be daunting.

Customers will feel as if they have the right to call out your weaknesses and judge you for them. That typical politeness with which we tend to treat each other goes away when you run a business, and it's sort of a no-holds-barred situation, where people can say whatever they like about you and your business. In normal relationships, that behavior isn't appropriate, but in a situation between a business and a customer, it has become common.

Customers may feel like they should have access to all the details of your business, including the history of the company. Beyond vulnerable, at times you might feel violated.

You can't control other people's behaviors, but you can control your responses. How you respond to vulnerability is witnessed by others, especially your employees, and it affects the company's culture. Your behavior sets the tone, and it's no different in these circumstances.

I've seen cultures develop at my companies where there's an operator or partner in charge of running the day-to-day operations. Since I'm marginally active at some of these businesses and visit them only occasionally, I get an objective view of the culture. These businesses reflect the personalities of the operator. For example, the employees at one business are very creative. The atmosphere is light and fun. The operator's annual conference was held at an artsy Airbnb in Denver that had a hipster vibe—just like the operator and the business. This particular leader has learned to manage his vulnerability, and it shows in the company's culture.

PROBLEMS EXPOSE WEAKNESSES

Problems seem to be drawn to weaknesses. This shouldn't come as a surprise. If you aren't good at something, you're going to have a problem with it eventually. At first, people will focus on the problem, but over time, that problem will draw attention to your weakness. Then the problem becomes attached to you. You've probably heard of the halo effect, where a person viewed in a positive light is always viewed that way, even when they're not a shining star. The other side of the coin is the horn effect. That's when you mess up and, going forward, people see you in a negative light. Now you're the person who's bad at whatever it is, no matter how good you become at that particular skill.

I experienced the horn effect, and it was not pleasant. An employee took some time off, and for some reason, I didn't understand when or why she was taking the time. I responded poorly, and for years, people aware of the situation expected me to respond poorly to any requests for time off. As ridiculous as that sounds, it happens, and it's very difficult to come back from. I wish I could have that one back.

Bear in mind that other people's perspectives don't represent "the truth." We all experience the world differently, based on previous experiences, biases, and other factors. This can become problematic because you have no control over people's past experiences. What they perceive as one thing may have nothing to do with what's really going on. A simple example would be you dressing a certain way that reminds them of someone they knew in the past who dressed that way too, and with whom they had a bad experience. Obviously, this doesn't portend a bad experience with you, but they might expect it.

In addition, customers and employees don't see the whole picture of your business, such as where you came from, what else you have going on, and where you're going. Each of us applies our own lens to a situation, and those lenses can vary greatly. While transparency matters, you can't invite everyone into the boardroom.

A better example is something that happened at the start of COVID, when I made a mistake—albeit with the best intentions—and my action was perceived much differently than I expected. With all the uncertainty surrounding the virus, people were worried about many things, including their jobs. To allay my employees' fears, I addressed them in a recorded video and sent it to each person in my company. The content was something like "Hey, I know we're all worried, but your job jobs are safe. We'll figure this thing out together and everyone will be okay. I know we'll come out of it bigger and better than before."

That was the gist of it—calm people down, let them know I'm there for them, and inspire confidence in the company and their jobs. Some employees appreciated the sentiment. Unfortunately, others heard something wildly different from what I intended. They were angry. One employee called to tell me he might quit. He had played the video on the speaker phone in his car while his young daughter listened from the back seat. She started crying and told her dad she was afraid he was going to die. I don't know how she got that impression (or what the man was thinking, playing a video in front of his child without first listening to it). Anyway, that act of support backfired spectacularly, and I'll never forget it.

When you run a business, your actions and words are amplified. Like anyone's actions and words, their interpretation varies among audience members. The wider the audience, the greater the odds of wild misinterpretation. So when you send a video to a hundred people, don't expect all of them to get it. Or forget it. No matter how many positive experiences people have with you—including your customers and employees—that one negative experience leaves a deeper, more lasting imprint. It will take many more positive ones for them to get past it.

LEADERSHIP MATTERS

I have flight anxiety, which is ironic considering how often I travel. On a flight from Boston to Phoenix, I was more relaxed than usual, listening to music and enjoying the pleasant flight. Suddenly, the plane hit some turbulence. It was strong enough that it caused a flight attendant to drop to her knees in the aisle. The sudden turbulence, paired with it knocking her down, caused my adrenaline to spike. As she stood up, we locked eyes. She smiled, made a comment about a "rough patch," and kept walking down the aisle like it was no big deal and certainly nothing she hadn't encountered before.

After freaking out in my head for a moment, I thought, "Wow, that's exactly how I feel sometimes!" Like the rug's been pulled out from under me and I have to put on a smile and pretend everything's A-OK.

This doesn't sound pleasant, right? But these kinds of experiences, the vulnerabilities they expose, and your responses to them will make or break you. They will make you a better leader, or they'll break your company.

You're going to make mistakes. You are a human being (right?). Real strength comes from admitting when you're wrong. People will have more confidence in someone who's willing to admit their mistakes. Gaslighting employees doesn't fool anyone, and it destroys any trust you've built. It may be hard to admit when you're wrong, but you'll sleep better at night, and people will respect your integrity. This takes having a thick skin, which is a given for business owners. Your thick skin will allow you to survive having your weaknesses exposed. Having a thick skin doesn't mean ignoring criticism. It does mean not taking people's opinions you don't agree with personally. It means being open to other people's perspectives and not punishing them for seeing things differently from you.

A thick skin allows you to have tough conversations with other people and, more importantly, with yourself.

In a typical relationship between peers, misunderstandings can be discussed and sorted out. It's different when you're in a position of authority. The power dynamic that exists between you and your staff requires you to take the high road and accept responsibility, even when your actions are misinterpreted. In the case of the video, I couldn't tell people it was their fault for not understanding my message. I had to take the blame and admit that I could have worded my messaging more carefully. I could have run it past a test group of employees to see how it would be perceived before blasting it out to the company. I should have taken into account my staff's situation and the intense fear they were experiencing, unfounded as it might have been. Especially for people who live paycheck to paycheck, the prospect of being out of work for even a short time can be terrifying. I did not consider any of that, but even if I had, and even if I had taken every step to ensure clarity, I would still have had to accept responsibility for the response. That's what a business owner does. That's leadership.

Some people avoid confrontations at all costs. They hide in their offices, ignoring emails, texts, and phone calls. This isn't an effective mode of operation for an employee. It's totally unacceptable for a business owner. We have to handle problems head-on and show people we're the leader they signed on to support. Over time, people's perspectives on you will change as you take on tougher challenges. You don't earn trust and confidence during the easy times. It's when things hit the fan that you show your true colors and hopefully show people you are up for the task. Getting past these challenges is the only way to move forward. Problems don't go away on their own, and if you ignore them, they could get worse. Take care of them, clear your mind, and move ahead.

Be vulnerable. Accept responsibility. Own your mistakes. Listen to what other people have to say and apologize if the situation warrants it. Falling on your sword is not a sign of weakness, but of strength and character. You might be surprised by how forgiving people can be when you're honest and willing to accept the blame for a bad situation. Deflecting, making excuses, and blaming others has the opposite effect.

As you scale your business, you'll become less vulnerable, largely due to the fact that you'll have layers of individuals between yourself and your employees and customers. They're more likely to look at the first line of authority instead of at you. Also, while you're growing, you're also improving the business so it runs like a well-oiled machine. Fewer mistakes means less scrutiny and criticism. With more resources, there are others to turn to for help. This is different from the situation of a new business owner, where everyone expects you to have all the answers.

VULNERABILITY IS MORE POWERFUL THAN PRIDE

You'll be vulnerable, and people will pounce on your vulnerabilities. Develop a thick skin and remind yourself that criticism usually isn't personal, but a reflection of the person's experiences and how they are perceiving your business and your actions within the business. Sometimes criticism is warranted, and you can learn from it. From *10x Is Easier than 2x*, "Research shows that highly hopeful and motivated people continually take feedback from not achieving their goals to iterate or adjust their pathway forward."[59] This is how you grow as a person and business leader, but you can't improve without putting yourself out there.

If we reframe how we look at vulnerability from "we've got a target on our backs" to "we may not like everything we hear, but we're going to use it to understand other people's perceptions, learn about ourselves, and turn our weaknesses into strengths," we'll set the example people want and need to see, given our positions. Model vulnerability and show people, especially employees, that it's okay to be imperfect. Hiding from your mistakes teaches them to do the same, creating a healthier, more open and honest culture free of judgment and shame.

---

59   Sullivan and Hardy, *10x*, 148.

PACK YOUR LUNCH QUESTIONS AND ACTIONS

1. On a scale from 1 to 10, how difficult is it for you to hear constructive criticism about your performance?
2. Do you believe that you can turn your weaknesses into strengths?
3. Have you had an experience where admitting a mistake or failure actually improved your reputation or opinion of others about you?

13

YOU WILL HAVE TO FACE SOME OF YOUR WORST FEARS

"He who is not every day conquering some fear has not learned the secret of life."

—RALPH WALDO EMERSON

I left a great job to start a business.

It's not like I left a job shoveling rocks in the Arizona desert—I was a lawyer. But I was chasing my dream, and so the day I gave notice at the law firm was exciting. I was so optimistic, looking forward to the next chapter in my life.

After giving my boss the news, I went back to my office. That's when reality set in. There I was, sitting in an air conditioned office full of furniture, hardware, software, and everything else I needed to do my job. I hadn't paid for any of it. I knew the job and knew there would be an automatic deposit into my bank account every other week, like clockwork. I started to question my decision. Was I being rash? Had I really thought this through? What if it didn't work out and I—gulp—failed? An uncomfortable feeling settled into my bones that I recognized as fear. Does this sound familiar?

My mind wandered, and I considered the worst-case scenario. If my business failed, I'd have to move my family from Michigan back to Arizona. I'd have to find another job. That might be a problem, since law firms invest a lot of time and training getting new lawyers up to speed, so they want to hire people who stick around. A new firm would want to know why I left the old one. They'd want to know what I'd been doing in the meantime too. What if I could never get a job again? That possibility wasn't likely, but still…I couldn't ignore it. Then there was my family to consider. What if they were unhappy in Michigan? What if I couldn't make enough money to support them?

I hadn't even launched my business, yet I was already freaking out about what would happen to my family *when it failed.*

I wondered if these fears were normal. Did every business owner go through this? If they did, how did they push through and overcome those fears to go on to start their businesses?

Entrepreneurs experience multiple fears when starting a business. Whether it's the fear of failure, change, or the unknown, each presents a challenge that can either motivate or cripple a business owner. Research suggests that fear acts as a psychological barrier that inhibits entrepreneurial growth, yet by confronting and transforming these fears into opportunities, entrepreneurs can thrive.[60] Therefore, acknowledging and managing fears—whether of failure, success, or inadequacy—is a crucial skill for sustaining and advancing a business in an uncertain environment.

We should spend less time thinking about what could go wrong and more time thinking about what could go right.

Recently, I heard a story about a firefighter who went into a burning building to rescue a woman. The woman lay on the floor in

60 Shivali Anand, "Seven Common Entrepreneurial Fears and How to Overcome Them—Early Growth," Early Growth, July 23, 2021, https://earlygrowthfinancialservices.com/blog/7-common-entrepreneurial-fears-and-how-to-overcome-them-early-growth/?utm_source=chatgpt.com.

the building, terrified. She wasn't injured, but she refused to get up. The firefighter tried to pick her up, but she fought him, kicking and screaming. He told her, "If you don't move, you're going to die." She responded, "I can't. I'm too scared!" He answered, "It's okay to be afraid. Be scared and do it anyway."

Entrepreneurs must face certain fears, such as fear of failure, fear of the unknown, fear of not having enough money, fear of letting people down, and—the worst fear of all—the fear of having to ask for our old jobs back. However, we can't allow these fears to hold us back. We must start before we're ready. By starting, we will become ready, and our fears will dissipate.

> It's okay to be afraid. Be scared
> and do it anyway.

I learned to push through my fears. They didn't go away entirely, but I didn't let them paralyze me. When fear overcomes you in business, accept it, but don't let it paralyze you. Be scared and do it anyway.

WORKING WITHOUT A SAFETY NET

Salaried employees, and even hourly ones, have safety nets. They get sick pay, vacation pay, insurance, retirement benefits, severance packages, and sometimes golden parachutes. Business owners have to pay for all of those things out of the company's profits. To top it off, they're the last people in the business to get paid.

When you leave a job to run a business, you fear not being able to get back to where you started, and not just financially. You could lose skills that you spent years developing. You lose connections with people. Your built-in network of coworkers disappears. You lose your old title and the accompanying prestige. This is especially painful if you leave a high-level job at a big company to start a small business where it's you and your admin sitting in a tiny office.

Quitting a job looks bad on your résumé. So does owning a business that fails. You fear never being able to get another job again if the whole business thing doesn't work out. You'll have to explain that big gap on your résumé, and that's not how you want to start an interview!

Fear of losing your social network is also common. Many people spend eight hours a day or more with dozens, sometimes hundreds of people they wouldn't have met if it weren't for their job. You get to know those people. You share stories and lunches, and you commiserate over shared problems. When you leave a job, those people don't come with you. This is another fear you can allay proactively by connecting with your coworkers outside of work and by developing a new social group that aligns with your new position as a business owner.

YOU HAVE EVERY RIGHT TO BE AFRAID

Fear is tied to limiting beliefs such as imposter syndrome. For the business owner, it's caused by the belief that we can't do the job. We worry that we're not smart enough, not educated enough, not experienced enough. Or just not tough enough to pull it off. We fear embarrassment too: What if my rotten brother-in-law was right, and I can't do this? What if I have to go crawling back to my old boss? Or—gasp—ask my parents for money?

Sometimes the unknown can be the worst. What's going to happen that I haven't considered? Tangible challenges we can deal with to a point. But those unknowns—our brains fill in the blanks with the worst possible scenario. The funny thing is that what happens is usually nowhere as bad as what we imagined.

People often think about the worst-case scenario because it's a natural protective mechanism ingrained in our brains, where uncertainty is interpreted as potential danger, leading us to anticipate negative outcomes as a way to prepare for potential threats, especially when facing new or uncertain situations. This is often called "catastrophizing."[61]

I was afraid that I wouldn't be able to provide for my family. I was going from a steady, secure, well-paying job with benefits to—what? I wasn't 100 percent sure. Yet I still wanted to go there! Since I was moving the whole family to Michigan, I couldn't keep my business plans a secret. "Yes, I really am quitting my job at the law practice and moving my family from sunny Arizona to Detroit. Why? Oh, didn't I tell you? I'm starting a bug business!"

You can imagine their reactions. My excitement quickly turned to doubt, then fear. Everyone thought I had lost my mind. But I clung to the commitment, knowing deep down that it was the right move for me. The idea of working for someone else every day, week after week and year after year, was the very definition of hell to me. Still, the fear lingered.

New fears arose in the days that followed. I was afraid of taking on the wrong partner and of hiring the wrong people. After all, we put our best faces forward when applying for work. But what did I really know about these people?

Not all these fears were unfounded. One of my employees turned out to be a chauvinist and a racist. Funny, he did not mention that on his résumé or during our interview. Before I figured it out, he had almost destroyed the culture of a call center and an operations center, a culture I had taken great pains to nurture. Worse, I let him stay on after I found out the truth. He'd come into my office with crocodile tears, apologizing for his behavior and promising to change. I can't believe, to this day, that I fell for his act. So a week after I saw who he was—a week too long, if you ask the people who worked alongside him—I let him go. The adage about being "slow to hire and quick to

61   Meg Jay, "What to Do When Your Mind (Always) Dwells on the Worst-Case Scenario," *Harvard Business Review*, September 15, 2020, https://hbr.org/2020/09/what-to-do-when-your-mind-always-dwells-on-the-worst-case-scenario.

fire" was a hard-learned lesson I'll never forget, but I still fear hiring someone like that again.

Once you identify your fears, take steps to avoid those worst-case scenarios. Dealing with my bad employee taught me to never be in a position where I had to hire someone quickly. Of course, sometimes things happen—an employee quits suddenly and without giving notice—and the pressure to hire quickly is unavoidable. But if you're paying attention, you know when business is picking up and there are clues that you'll be needing more people. Start looking sooner rather than later. Another scenario I vowed to avoid was allowing one mistake to turn into two mistakes. My second mistake was not firing the guy quickly enough. I vowed to not repeat that error.

BE AFRAID AND KEEP GOING

When I was studying for the bar exam, my wife, who was pregnant with our first child, began having severe health issues. She developed pregnancy-induced cardiomyopathy, which is a form of heart disease. She was only thirty, though, and the condition added to the stress of carrying a child. I worried about her, picked up on her stress, and struggled to study. I had paid over a thousand dollars for a guided study course, which promised to help me prepare for the exam. I was supposed to attend a daily lecture and complete the assignments. Well, that lasted exactly one day. I spent the rest of the time in the hospital looking after my wife and then our son.

I worried about the exam, especially since I didn't take two critical courses in law school, Secured Transactions and Commercial Paper, which were both heavily tested on the bar. I remember sitting on a cot in the intensive care unit with a pile of books, cramming for the test. My wife's health improved, thankfully, but I went into the exam worried and left it even more concerned, convinced I'd failed. Unbelievably, I passed the bar!

More importantly, I survived the stress of a very sick wife and the birth of my first son. The exam, in comparison, was easier. Still, I was amazed that I could go through that experience, study for a very difficult exam, and actually pass. But honestly, the real rock star of the entire experience was my wife. I had never been more proud of, more impressed by, and more in love with her.

PACK YOUR LUNCH, FEARLESSLY

I coach other business owners, and they often share their fears with me. Usually, those fears make sense, because I've had them myself. Sometimes, though, my clients come to me with fears that are, to me, a little outrageous. One of my clients was afraid he'd have to live on less than $150,000 a year. Mind you, he didn't live in New York City or Silicon Valley. He could support his family on much less money, but he did not want to sacrifice his lifestyle for the business. That scared him. In my mind, if he couldn't sacrifice some of his expenditures—which were essentially luxuries—he'd end up sacrificing something more important in the end. Like his business. He wasn't willing to pack his lunch...

Face your fears, but be realistic about them. Is what you fear really so scary? Are your expectations in line with reality?

Resolving to overcome your fears can only come after you start. The woman struggling to hire a manager for her rock climbing gym feared hiring the wrong person, but she had to overcome that fear, hire the best candidate for the job, and manage the situation from that point. If she waited for that fear to go away, she never would have hired anyone.

Once you begin tackling your fears, you'll often find they are not as scary as you thought. They're rarely unsurmountable. The unknown is scary, but when you put a face on it, and you confront that face, it becomes manageable—and less scary. You will learn so much about yourself and what you're capable of doing. You will surprise yourself. With every fear conquered, you'll gain confidence to tackle the next one. Facing your fears about starting a business gives you the courage to do it, which is something most people will never do. It empowers you to make your dreams come true instead of living out someone else's dream.

Face your fears. You will learn so much about yourself and what you're capable of doing.

In a way, fear is not so much your opponent as your partner. It's a reaction to new challenges, and without those challenges, you can't improve. So welcome fear into your life. See it for what it is. See what it's trying to "protect" you from, or rather, hold you back from. You are in the driver's seat. Relegate fear to the passenger seat and allow it to serve its purpose, not as a navigator, but as a sign that you are onto something bigger and better.

Facing your fears opens the door to launching a business and building the life you want. You'll build confidence with each new challenge, and though the fear will persist, you'll be better equipped to handle it.

PACK YOUR LUNCH QUESTIONS AND ACTIONS

1. When was a time that you made a decision out of fear and regretted it?
2. What is your biggest fear about starting a business?
3. Is the fear of *not* starting a business scarier to you than the fear of starting one?

14

YOU WILL HAVE FAILURES

"The very first company I started failed with a great bang. The second one failed a little bit less, but still failed. The third one, you know, proper failed, but it was kind of okay. I recovered quickly. Number four almost didn't fail. It still didn't really feel great, but it did okay. Number five was PayPal."

—MAX LEVCHIN

Before I went to law school and became a lawyer, and before I quit being a lawyer to start my "first" business, I had another first business. I don't talk about it much because it failed miserably. Freedom Pest Control was the business I tried to start with my brother. I spent a lot of money on licensing, logos, and other stuff I thought was important, and some of it was. But I underestimated some other things that turned out to be more important. My brother and I were young and immature, and we butted heads. Undercapitalized and disorganized, we were destined for failure from the start.

The failure surprised me. I thought starting a business would be easy, like we'd take all the necessary steps and the customers and money would roll in. But there were a lot of steps, from licensing to building a website, getting an office and equipment, and then doing the actual work. Baking the muffins or, in our case, controlling the pests. And the world, to my dismay, did not sit up, take notice, and applaud me for all my hard work! Every day there was more to do and little satisfaction. And no one noticed.

The word "failure" has a negative connotation, and because of that, I seldom use it. Failure sounds so final, like something you can't recover from. You can recover from most things, so I prefer terms like "hurdle" and "setback." Hurdles and setbacks aren't final.

I look at that first business as a setback. Seven years later, I tried again. That business was successful, and over ten years later, it's still going strong.

Failure insinuates finality. It implies that nothing good came from the attempt. As if running a business for a while was a complete waste of time, money, and effort. Since starting that first company, my mentality toward failure has changed completely. Failure is trying. Failure is learning. Failure leads to success. If it weren't for the many mini failures and micro mistakes I made, I wouldn't have the successful businesses I have today. To me, failure only happens when I give up, and giving up is a personal decision within my control. So failure doesn't *happen* to me. It doesn't make me its victim. I survey the situation and decide whether or not to move on. Like Nelson Mandela said, "I never lose. I either win, or I learn." You can do the same. Don't allow failure to "happen" to you. Don't let it make you its victim.

Don't allow failure to "happen" to you.
Don't let it make you its victim.

Changing our perspective toward failure allows us to learn about ourselves. We learn from our mistakes. We also learn how resilient we are. We might sustain a huge loss, but as long as we keep going and rebuild, we can do it better next time, knowing that another failure won't take us down.

FAIL FAST ON A SCALE YOU CAN AFFORD AND MOVE ON

Modern corporations encourage their people to fail fast. They can afford to have multiple failures. They recover, fail again, and continue until they get the technology or product right. Most companies don't have the luxury of that approach, but they can still choose to fail on a smaller scale.

Failure isn't final. It's usually not as bad as you think. By realizing the benefits of making mistakes and even failing, you can leverage what you learn for future success. Success is not built upon the foundation of success. Success is built upon the foundation of failure. Start by changing your perspective and inviting failures into your life for what they have to offer. If a thriving business fell into your lap with perfect employees and customers, along with a detailed playbook for running the business—and an operating manager to run the place for you—what would you have accomplished? What would you learn? It's only by trying, failing, learning from failure, and trying again that we can improve and succeed.

We build our entire lives upon failure. That sounds really dark, but think about your relationships. Think about the mistakes you've made with partners, spouses, and children and how you learn from each mistake and try to be better. I wasn't a perfect parent when I started a family. No one is. I yelled when I shouldn't have and was too lenient when I should have been stricter. I had to give myself the grace to make mistakes, knowing they weren't the last word on the parent I would become.

> Success is not built upon the
> foundation of success. Success is built
> upon the foundation of failure.

Like they say, "Easy come, easy go." According to Anne Kates Smith in *Kiplinger*, "Studies have found that 70% of the time, family assets are lost from one generation to the next, and assets are gone 90% of the time by the third generation."[62] We've all seen the stories of celebrity kids who get into all kinds of trouble. They have everything given to them and don't have a chance to fail. But how can they learn without failing? When you earn money and success, you treat it differently. You value it, knowing what it took to get there.

SUCCESS BUILT ON FAILURE

Companies are built on failures. Before Microsoft was a household name, Bill Gates, Paul Allen, and a man named Paul Gilbert started Traf-O-Data. They created traffic reports and sold them to customers. When the government began providing this data for free, their business became obsolete. Presumably Gilbert left the partnership because the failure was too much for him, but Gates and Allen rose from the ashes of Traf-O-Data to create one of the most famous tech companies of all time.

---

62 Anne Kates Smith, "Five Strategies to Keep Your Heirs from Blowing Their Inheritance," Kiplinger, last updated August 19, 2024, https://www.kiplinger.com/article/saving/t021-c000-s002-5-strategies-keep-heirs-from-blowing-inheritance.html.

Before they made it big, some of the most legendary people in the world failed. Not once or twice, but many times.

Thomas Edison: According to his records, Edison failed 2,774 times before creating a working design of an electric light bulb.[63]

Michael Jordan was cut from his high school basketball team, lost over three hundred games, and missed twenty-six game-winning shots. Jordan has said, "I have failed over and over and over again in my life. And that is why I succeed."[64]

Stephen King received thirty rejections for his first book, *Carrie*.[65]

To the outsider, people who came out on top often appear to be overnight successes. More often, they've been working at the game for years and suffered many failures. Working through failure takes grit. You have to be willing to learn from each failure and keep going.

It's common for an entrepreneur to start three or more businesses before one becomes successful. For example, a survey by Hiscox found that entrepreneurs, on average, experienced 3.8 failures before achieving success.[66]

WHEN ONE DOOR CLOSES, ANOTHER ONE OPENS

What seems like a failure in the moment may be a blessing in disguise in hindsight. I took the LSAT in 2008. I did well enough to get into

63 Puja Roy, "How Many Times Thomas Failed? Know Edison's Marvellous and Lesser Known Inventions," Vedantu, November 22, 2022, https://www.vedantu.com/blog/how-many-times-edison-failed-to-invent-bulb.

64 Alicia Behar, "7 Famous People Who Failed a Lot Before They Succeeded," SkyPrep, June 4, 2021, https://skyprep.com/2021/06/04/7-famous-people-who-failed-a-lot-before-they-succeeded/.

65 Behar, "7 Famous People."

66 Einar H. Dyvik, "Share of Possible Entrepreneurs with Fear of Failure Worldwide 2023, by Country," Statista, July 4, 2024, https://www.statista.com/statistics/268788/fear-of-failure-start-ups-in-leading-economic-nations/.

the vast majority of law schools in the United States, but not Brigham Young University, where I had earned my undergraduate degree. I had my heart set on BYU and was severely disappointed. Despite scholarship offers from other schools, I refused to give up on my dream school. So I took a year off and studied hard. I paid for a professional tutoring course and invested hundreds of additional hours. I retook the LSAT—and scored one point lower than the first time! Suffice it to say, I didn't get into BYU. That failure hit hard, and it stuck with me for years.

One night I was sitting around a campfire, telling my buddies that story, and one of them asked, "If you had received your law degree at BYU, would your life be any different from the way it is now?"

I had to think about it. Without a crystal ball, I could only surmise how going to Arizona State differed from BYU in the big scheme of things. Considering how well everything turned out and how happy I was at that moment, I couldn't imagine going back in time and changing anything. Thinking about it that way made me very grateful for my test results. Ironically, by the time I graduated, Arizona State was ranked twenty-sixth-best and BYU was ranked the thirty-ninth-best law school in the US.[67] The ranking may have changed since, but back then, that high ranking gave me a lot of satisfaction.

Failures can be blessings in disguise. They can be building blocks toward towering successes. Only by trying and failing will we ever know the outcomes. Without trying and risking failure, we won't know or grow. That was the first major failure of my adult life, and there would be many more. I'd like to think it toughened me up for what was to come. Sixteen years later, if I were to fail a test, I doubt whether I'd lose any sleep over it.

Potential failures are less intimidating if you change your perspective and see them as experiments. Before going to law school, I earned a degree in chemistry. That science requires conducting experiments and observing the results. You might have a theory as to what you believe will

---

67   "U.S. News Rankings (with +/-) from 2012/2013," Spivey Consulting, February 16, 2013, https://www.spiveyconsulting.com/blog-post/us-news-rankings-with-from-20122013/.

happen, but until you conduct the experiment, you have no certainty and no proof. Most of the time in chemistry, you prove that your theory is wrong. That's just the way it goes—it's typical scientific methodology.

The same process applies in business. You have a vision, goals, and a plan to meet them, but you never know how that plan will play out until you put it into action. Then you observe the results, good or bad, and try the next thing. Is that a failure? Or simply an experiment that delivered new information? Sometimes outcomes point us in a new and better direction, perhaps toward success.

New entrepreneurs do not think this way, but they can shift their perspectives to view every failure as a success or a stepping stone toward success. Each experience, or experiment, allows you to develop your next level of genius, which could benefit you more than whatever was in your original plan. Failure builds acceptance and resilience. It stimulates curiosity.

Failure carries a connotation of finality, but in business, failures aren't final. They're part of the process. Thinking of them as "the end" can create a self-fulfilling prophecy, which is why it's so important to shift our mindsets from the start.

Focusing on failure can drive you to fail. This concept played out perfectly on a family rafting trip. Our guide told us about a difficult section coming up ahead where rafts often got stuck and sometimes overturned, dumping rafters into the rushing white water. I asked him how he would keep us safe, and he told us this story:

"Well, I always had trouble with that spot, and I'm very experienced. So when a new guide joined the crew, I was worried that he'd lose control of his raft there. I didn't get a chance to talk to him about it and was amazed to find out that even on his first trip, he navigated the river flawlessly. So I asked him if the other guides had given him some tips to keep himself and his party safe.

"He said that no one told him about that dangerous spot. Instead, the other guide that day only told him exactly where to guide the raft, and so that's what he focused on. He didn't realize that by focusing on the right path he had totally avoided the dangerous one."

If you are always focused on what can go wrong, you could end up guiding yourself in that direction. Instead, focus on what could go right and aim your business in that direction.

FAILURES AS TRAINING FOR THE FUTURE

While working toward my undergraduate degree at Brigham Young University, I was planning on becoming a dentist. That plan didn't work out. But the required chemistry course taught me to see business failures as experiments, and the insights gained as worth the risk. My legal career taught me to be a critical thinker and analyze situations from all angles beyond my natural perspective. It gave me the negotiation and communication skills I needed to be a successful entrepreneur.

In legal practices, the bulk of policies and contracts are developed from what is learned through failure. Say you have a customer contract detailing services to be provided, and the customer doesn't pay for the service for whatever reason. As a lawyer, you revisit the contract to see if that situation is covered. If it isn't, you change the contract going forward. This is a typical job for a transactional attorney who writes contracts. The best contract lawyers have read, written, and revised many contracts. They've seen so many mistakes that they know what people tend to leave out that can get them into trouble.

Oddly enough, when I tell someone I left my legal profession to start a business, they automatically see my career move as a failure. I see it as finding a better way to use my talents. I certainly enjoy the way my life turned out, and I have no complaints or regrets.

Experiencing small failures and learning from them can help you avoid catastrophic failures. In *Good to Great*, author and entrepreneur Jim Collins calls this strategy "firing bullets before cannonballs." Collins notes that he aims with bullets, which don't use a lot of resources, before firing the game-changing cannonballs.[68]

---

68   Jim Collins, *Good to Great: Why Some Companies Make the Leap...and Others Don't* (Harper Business, 2001).

For example, say you're not sure how to invest revenue into your business for the best return. Maybe you should put it into marketing, but what type of marketing? You could spend a bundle on one type only to discover it's not right for your services and market. Or you could shoot some bullets at a few types, see what works, and then fire your cannonballs.

IT'S YOUR RESPONSIBILITY

As the leader of your business, failures at any level are your responsibility. At my pest control business, safety is a critical concern, so anytime there's a safety issue, I jump on a call with the CEO, the regional manager, the branch manager, and the individual involved in the incident. Even though I wasn't at a site or on the road when it occurred, I have to know what happened, and it's up to me to resolve the issue and ensure it doesn't happen again. I take problems like those very seriously. Did we hire the wrong person? Train them improperly? Or are our protocols out of date? Did we miss something? Regardless, I consider it my personal failure, and I set out to correct the problem. Business owners who own the failures as well as the successes are more likely to earn the respect and loyalty of their employees. They'll also have greater business success because they'll be open to learning from the failure and applying that learning on a wider scale.

When you take ownership, you take control of your life. When you blame other people and force ownership of the failure on them, you give up control. See failures as opportunities for improvement and leverage them as such. Otherwise, they truly are failures.

Owning failures sets the standard for your people too. Employees who see you unafraid to admit mistakes will be more open about their own mistakes. This is how you create a culture of transparency and trust where your people can thrive unburdened with the fear of being "found out" for every mistake they're afraid to disclose.

When you take ownership, you take
control of your life. When you blame
other people and force ownership of the
failure on them, you give up control.

PACK YOUR LUNCH FOR FAILURES
THAT LEAD TO SUCCESSES

Failures are a sacrifice you make to learn and grow as a person and business owner. Adopting a different perspective of failures and equating them to learning and growth is a powerful tool that will move you ahead more quickly than avoiding them. Learn to get excited about the prospect of failures and what they will teach you.

As you're pulling yourself up from a failure, remind yourself, "This is why I have what it takes to make it when most other people don't. This is what makes me unique—a special type of person within that small percentage of people who choose becoming an entrepreneur over being an employee. I'm built different."

You can tolerate what others cannot. You're more resilient, and you see the opportunity in failure. You take responsibility and take charge.

I sometimes use personality assessments in my businesses to figure out where people's strengths lie, what motivates them, how they learn, and where they are most prone to succeed. Depending on the test, they can be very insightful, telling you things about yourself and others that you didn't realize.

I took one myself recently. Afterward, I met with the administrator to get my results. She looked at me across the desk, and I could tell she was uncomfortable. She couldn't look me in the eye. Naturally, I was worried. What horrible things had she uncovered in my test responses?

Finally, she spoke up. "Allan," she said, "I don't know how to tell you this, but…"

"Yes?" I asked.

"Well, according to your scores, you're totally unemployable!"

I LOLed. Maybe I should have been offended. But I wasn't. I was flattered because she was right. I wasn't cut out to be an employee, and so it's a darned good thing I chose this career path.

In an interview with Howard Stern, comedian Jerry Seinfeld said, "Your blessing in life is when you find the torture you're comfortable with."[69] For some people, that misery is working for someone else. For me, it's being a business owner and facing failure (read *lessons*) over and over. And I wouldn't trade it for anything else in the world.

PACK YOUR LUNCH QUESTIONS AND ACTIONS

1. What failure in your life are you most proud of?
2. How have failures helped you develop into who you are today?
3. Have you ever considered that *not* doing something could also be seen as a failure?

69 Jerry Seinfeld, "Jerry Seinfeld on Finding 'The Torture You're Comfortable With,'" interview by Howard Stern, posted June 9, 2023, by Screen Off Script,YouTube, https://www.youtube.com/watch?v=v79gTLkudns&ab_channel=ScreenOffScript.

CONCLUSION

"A journey of a thousand miles begins with a single step."

—CHINESE PROVERB

You chose this book because there's something inside you that wants to build something great. You want to create something. You're capable of achieving that goal. But you won't get there without sacrifices. By packing your lunch—making minor yet necessary sacrifices up front-—you'll reap major rewards in the long run. You'll also avoid making major sacrifices that are inevitable if you don't plan ahead, identify your nonnegotiables, and protect them.

I underestimated what it took to be a business owner. I made the wrong sacrifices. I made mistakes. I had failures. You'll do the same thing, but you'll do it less because of what you've learned from my experiences.

You were no doubt surprised to learn about the many sacrifices required to be an entrepreneur. I guarantee that being aware of the sacrifices and mindful enough to make the short-term sacrifices will save you a lot of pain down the road.

You will make sacrifices.

You will take risks.

You will sacrifice your financial security.

You'll have less time for hobbies.

Your relationships will change.

You'll learn to avoid distractions and to deal with conflict.

You'll have stress, feel out of control, and feel lonely.

You will learn to be flexible with your identity and be vulnerable.

You'll face your worst fears, you'll fail, and you'll get up and try again.

You'll be scared to death at times, but you'll be a business owner. And like me, you won't want to trade it for anything in the world.

READY, SET, GO

I hope you start your business. If you have a business, I hope you found what you needed in this book to scale it, and if you want to start another business, I hope you do that too. You now know the sacrifices you need to make. And perhaps more importantly, you now know all of the success that comes only by making them. Make them wisely and reap the long-term rewards.

Now get moving. Your greatest potential is just on the other side of sacrifice.

For more info about getting to the next level, check out the resources at allandraper.com. Connect with via my website, follow me on social media, follow my podcast, subscribe to my newsletter, and if you need one-on-one guidance, schedule a call with me. If you're looking for an angel investor, I might be interested. If you need a speaker for your corporate or organizational event, I might be interested in that too. The links are located on the last page of this book, and I'm just a click away.

ACKNOWLEDGMENTS

Jules, without you I am nothing. Thank you for being my biggest (and sometimes only) fan.

"Come what may, she believes and that faith is something I've never known before."

Maddox, Jaxon, Olivia, you are my legacy and my reason for shooting for the stars. Soon it will be your turn.

Mom, you would do anything for your children, and at times you were asked to. Thank you.

My dad. Long gone but not forgotten. Thank you for the entrepreneurial drive that I cannot seem to get out of my system.

Colleen, Derrick, Kevin, Brent, and Tasha, somehow we survived with eight of us in a three-bedroom, one-bathroom house. The backyard smelled like urine because sometimes the wait for the bathroom was just too much. We always blamed it on the animals, but deep down we know that's not true. We somehow survived. That would not have been possible without you.

Brent, my first business partner. The road to success has been anything but smooth. Thanks for taking a chance on me.

Matt, ride or die. Thanks for staying the course when it was difficult to see. Homies for life.

Mat, thank you for teaching me that relationships are first and business is second. Thanks for the patience. Thanks for believing.

Thank you Hunter, Jake, Jana, and Eric. I don't show up for a lot of meetings, but the ones I do show up for, at least I immediately take them over and disrupt the agenda. Thanks for the partnership. Thanks for the vision.

Thomas and Josh. Thank you. Without you, my dream of owning a law firm would have been left unfulfilled.

Ian, John, Aaron, Tony, Christian, Kenny, thank you for your sacrifices that allowed me to be part of your journey.

To my former business partners. I still have a relationship with some of you. With others, I don't. I learned a lot from you and enjoyed the journey. With some of you, I could have done things differently. You know who you are. I promise to do better.

Tori, thank you for everything you do, because it feels like you literally do everything.

Susan, this book would not be possible without you. Thank you.

Presidente Tanner—you showed me that someone could love God, love his family, and build a business empire without sacrificing what matters most.

I want to thank *everyone* that has ever thanked me for posting a video or sharing something with them. For years, my thoughts and words fell on deaf ears, and it bothered me. Then I realized that I was doing it all for "the one" anyway. For you.

I also want to thank the "haters." The ones that tried to discourage me and bring me down. I learned so much about myself from these interactions. I learned a lot about my *why*. I turned your negative words into fuel.

And last but always first, I want to thank God. Anything and everything that I am and that I have ever achieved is thanks to Him.

ABOUT THE AUTHOR

ALLAN DRAPER is a serial entrepreneur, investor, wealth builder, business growth expert, attorney, and host of the successful podcast *The Business Growth Pod*. He specializes in motivating entrepreneurs to make short-term sacrifices to build businesses and wealth.

Allan is passionate and dedicated to helping others avoid sacrificing what matters most for that which matters less. He has contributed to the success of numerous startups, such as Proof Pest Control, Lizard Marketing, Ernst, Brown & Draper, Bug Bux, and others. Since Proof's inception in 2015, it has taken over the market for quality service, with fourteen locations in seven states. Proof now has a market valuation of approximately $100 million.

Through Allan's various companies, he employs hundreds of individuals. He doesn't just see his employees as workers, but as family. One of the reasons that Allan builds companies is to facilitate the professional and personal growth of others.

Serving the community has remained a primary mission for Allan and one of his core values in business. One of the tenets Allan lives by is giving away a significant portion of his wealth to benefit others. Practicing what he preaches, and wanting to show others the benefits of helping out, Allan helped found Proof Gives Back, a nonprofit organization dedicated to volunteerism and serving those in need across the country.

Allan's diverse industry experiences, successes, and even failures have led him to become a mentor and coach to business owners and entrepreneurs. Allan's passion for wanting others to succeed is a driving force for him, and this has led him to offer business consultations, legal reviews, and financial planning services to other entrepreneurs and businesses for free.

Allan's podcast *The Business Growth Pod* offers listeners advice from CEOs and industry leaders who share insights and personal experience on marketing, personnel, hiring, management scaling, and other aspects related to business operations. Allan's podcast also gives insight into how he has achieved success and what he can do to help you build something great. His weekly podcast has received nearly one hundred thousand downloads, with audiences across forty different countries.

When Allan is not playing sports or coaching one of his three children—Maddox, Jaxon, and Olivia—he enjoys reading, playing golf, and fly-fishing.

Allan is married to the love of his life, Julianna. They live in Arizona.

Website: https://allandraper.com/
Instagram: @realallandraper
YouTube: @allandraper
X: @allanrdraper
LinkedIn: www.linkedin.com/in/allanrdraper
Facebook: www.facebook.com/allan.draper.1
Calendly: https://calendly.com/allandraper